Age Different Relationships

Age Different Relationships

Finding Happiness with an Older or Younger Love

JACK MUMEY

AND

CYNTHIA TINSLEY

DEACONESS PRESS
Minneapolis, Minnesota

Published by Deaconess Press (a service of Fairview
Riverside Medical Center, a division of Fairview Hospital and
Healthcare Services), 2450 Riverside Avenue South,
Minneapolis, MN 55454

Library of Congress Cataloging-in-Publication Data

Mumey, Jack.
  Age different relationships : finding happiness with an older
or younger love / Jack Mumey and Cynthia Tinsley.
      p.   cm.
  Includes bibliographical references.
  ISBN 0-925190-65-9 (pbk.)
  1. Man-woman relationships.   I. Tinsley, Cynthia.   II. Title.
HQ801.M84   1993
306.7–dc20   93-16877
                                                                        CIP

First printing: April, 1993

Printed in the United States of America
97 96 95 94 93   7 6 5 4 3 2 1

Cover design by Robert P. Sedlack

Publisher's Note: Deaconess Press publishes books and
other materials related to the subjects of physical health,
mental health, and chemical dependency. Its publications,
including *Age Different Relationships,* do not necessarily reflect
the philosophy of Fairview Hospital and Healthcare Services
or their treatment programs.

For all the couples who have taken the plunge into an Age Different Relationship with courage and conviction, defying what before may have seemed impossible.

And to my coauthor, without whose love, spirit of adventure, and courage to change, neither this book nor our relationship would have been possible.

those who danced
were thought to be quite insane
by those who couldn't hear the music
                    —anonymous

---

i do not expect you
            to take care of me
i promise you i will
            take care of myself
                    —Cynthia Tinsley

Contents

Acknowledgments .... *ix*

Introduction *by Jack Mumey* .... *xi*

Introduction *by Cynthia Tinsley* .... *xv*

One   Spanning the Years *1*

Two   Finances: Your Checkbook or Mine? *11*

Three   Sex: A New Look at an Old Subject *33*

Four   Children: Yours, Mine, or Ours? *51*

Five   Ghost Partners, Part 1: Previous Mates *67*

Six   Ghost Partners, Part 2: Previous Lovers *79*

Seven   Housekeeping: The Great Battleground *91*

Eight   Marriage vs. Playing House *101*

Nine   In-Laws and Other Relations *113*

Ten   Careers: Yours and Mine *121*

Eleven   Friends: Getting Them, Keeping Them, ... *133*
          Losing Them

Afterword *by Jack Mumey* *147*

Afterword *by Cynthia Tinsley* *149*

Acknowledgments

So many people have touched our lives in the writing of this book; new friends we have made, and those with whom we renewed bonds after losing touch with them.

We heartily applaud the magnificent and brave performances of our extended families: Jack's in Denver, and Cynthia's in both Lubbock, Texas, and Philadelphia. They have demonstrated great patience and love in not appearing bored to death when we went on and on about our project. They asked all the right questions and gave the right answers to us when we needed them. Their support has been gratefully received, and we thank them for it.

Our Senior Editor at Deaconess, Jack Caravela, has been faithfully loyal to this project for more than a year. He believed it could happen and guided it to its fruition, carefully avoiding bruising two egos while giving the sense of direction and purpose to the book that we sought and, hopefully, achieved.

Ed Wedman, Editor-in-Chief at Deaconess Press, was our launching pad with the Editorial Board, and without his support, this book would simply not have happened.

Finally, to all the age different couples who sat through breakfasts with us, hardly being allowed to eat as we bombarded them with the most intimate questions about their relationships, a special thanks. Without their enthusiasm and candor, both in the written surveys and the personal interviews, this book would not have been possible.

Both authors' colleagues at their respective workplaces could not have been more supportive and willing to take up the slack when either of us found it necessary to "go off writing," or when we presented them with something less than our best side because we were struggling over a chapter or an idea or two.

"We thank ya'll for hangin' in," as Cyn would say.

Or, "Thanks, group," as Jack would say.

Do we detect an age difference there?

Introduction
by Jack Mumey

We have an outstanding and rewarding relationship, my coauthor and I. Our relationship is full of the pleasures of warmth and humor, of caring and understanding, of support and constructive criticism.

Our relationship is sensitive and sensual, nurturing and natural, comfortable and loving in every respect. Those are some of the pleasures of our relationship.

There are pitfalls, too. We don't agree on some issues of concern to both of us. What we have managed to do is find tools and methods to resolve the difficult issues and to build on the pleasures.

This is what our book is all about: the pleasures and the pitfalls of an age different relationship. These prefaces and our afterwords will be the only times we will speak to our readers with separate voices. (We should mention, however, that the poetry at the beginning of each chapter is "original Cyn.") What you will read in the rest of this book is the result of our months of research with other age different couples. We will blend that research with our own experiences and with those of my patients with whom I have had the pleasure of working over the years at Gateway Treatment Center in Denver, Colorado.

The question asked by most people with whom we have talked, and by friends and acquaintances whose curiosity finally gets the best of them, is, "What *is* the age difference between you two?"

My standard answer has been much the same with people who have inquired about the number of years of my sobriety. Namely, "What makes that important to you?"

After the dust has settled a little from this rhetorical jousting, the truth is we'll never tell! The reason? It simply doesn't matter. We have concentrated on the quality of our relationship and the elements we each have brought with us to the marriage. This quality and these elements have made our relationship very special and very different from previous experiences we each have passed through.

I am confident I did not give in to the myth of "midlife crisis." I say "myth" because, as a therapist, I do not believe such a dynamic occurs for men (although many men have been labeled with it and even use it themselves when they suddenly leave long-standing marriages and take up with a partner many years their junior).

"Midlife crisis," I think, is a convenient excuse for irresponsible behavior and, perhaps, a very vain attempt to blame waning sexuality on the existing marriage.

I am equally confident that my wife Cyn was not looking for another father. She has a very nice father already, thank you, and the relationship between us is mutually rewarding.

So assuage your curiosity with the fact that there is enough of a difference between us to warrant the both of us committing to change; change that means a new way of thinking and acting and planning and building our lives together without giving up the individual personalities we are.

One of the activities we have come to share and enjoy is spotting other couples and commenting, "There's an age different relationship!" Perhaps we get such a kick out of this because we know that a strong age different relationship is a special thing. What makes these relationships special is what we will share with you in the following pages. Our aim is to have you look at ideas that may at first seem outside accepted norms, yet hold all sorts of possibilities for discovery.

Somewhere a special someone might be waiting; a some-one who may span a different decade or two, or even represent a generational gap, yet who beckons with the promise of stability and love. This may be someone who brings a deep sense of personal commitment to the success of your relationship.

I encourage you to keep an open mind; explore with us the pleasures and the pitfalls. Let us help you enhance the former and build safe bridges over the latter.

The rewards are enormous. You might even find that the word "fun" has crept ever so subtly back into your life. Now, really, would that upset you?

Introduction
by Cynthia Tinsley

The draft of my preface has salad dressing spilled all over it, and I wrote it on some unused pages sent along with my last Day-Timer order. It is somewhat difficult to read.

My coauthor, on the other hand, regularly folds his socks, and would probably iron his underwear if there were space in the house to set up the ironing board.

I wrote my preface in salad dressing at 11:00 p.m. He wrote his at 4:30 a.m. I'm not even human at that hour, and he's dead to the world after about 9:00 p.m.

Some of our differences may have something to do with a difference in age. Many have to do with differences in personality. All relationships suffer these pitfalls; a significant age difference in partners simply adds another dimension to what all couples face.

Let's talk about age different relationships. Older man, younger woman—she's a "gold digger." Younger man, older woman—he's looking for a new mother image. Same age friends of the older partner may treat the younger as a child, while the peers of the younger partner may assume that the older one is hopelessly out of date with their point of view. We have read much about younger partners looking for a surrogate parent and older partners looking for a return to youth or, at worst, for fantasy fulfillment of incest or a child substitute.

However, there is another side to the story of age different relationships. Sometimes our preconceived notions limit what we believe to be our options. This happens in relationships as well in as other areas of our lives. In reality, sometimes we are more mature than our years, and feel more comfortable with those older than we are. Sometimes we are younger-thinking that our peers, and identify more closely with those younger than us. Although we will debate the issue in the course of this book, physiological studies indicate women reach their sexual peak later than men—by several years. My personal belief is that many men of my own age may feel threatened by a "new woman" such as myself, a woman who is ambitious, assertive, determined to make a good life for herself and her family.

As a society, our family values and lifestyles have changed. The issue is how we are adapting to these changes. Extended families are practically the norm, considering divorce, remarriage, and children of current and previous relationships. Then, when we add issues such as a new husband or wife being the same age as children of a previous marriage, we have problems with which we have seldom dealt before. These are not easy issues, nor do we often speak about them as a society.

In this book, we will speak about these issues and others. We will address the joys, the surprises, the advantages of age different relationships. We will also address the pitfalls, the difficulties, the challenges of age different relationships. We will note that all relationships have such joys and pitfalls.

We will, most of all, make the point that two people know when they belong together, and that commonly held interpretations of relationships are often functions of biases, from socialization or from personal experience. Our focus is on age different relationships, but the same principles apply to color different or culture different relationships.

As coauthor of this book, my position is as follows: we live in a new age. We are challenging many of our traditional values and are increasingly prepared to part with traditions when we find they stand in the way of our happiness. Choosing to be with someone older or younger by several years may be breaking with tradition, but doing so may also allow a satisfying and rewarding relationship.

Most of you reading this book remember when man first set foot on the moon. What might it be like to be in a relationship with a person who does not remember that event? Someone who grew up knowing the planets were within our reach? I know people who have spoken from personal experience about the bombing of Pearl Harbor during World War II. What might it be like to be in a relationship with someone who has lived through such an event? (Those of us who have older or younger friends know that age different relationships are not limited to those of an intimate nature, although those intimate relationships are the focus of this book. Still, it is important that we not deny ourselves the rewards of age different friendships as well.)

We are creatures committed to change, whether we acknowledge it or not. It is true that as a society we have committed many errors, even crimes. We are also creatures created by God, however you conceive God. And again as a society, we have done many, many good deeds. We are working to save the environment for future generations. We are working to make the world a peaceful place; struggling, sometimes with great difficulty, but working nevertheless. We are working very hard to include the disabled, the underabled, and other groups against which we have previ-

xvii

ously discriminated as contributing, useful members of society.

As individuals, we deserve happiness and fulfillment as human beings. Sometimes, happiness and fulfillment are achieved outside of societal norms. One example of this is the age different relationship.

While age different relationships are the subject of this book, its underlying goals are to offer tools to achieve satisfaction, the pursuit of a fully-lived life, and the potential to be fully human. At times, achievement of these goals requires stepping outside the boundaries of what we have always accepted. Please, enjoy the book. Feel free to expand your options.

Expanding options—also known as exercising freedom—is the purpose of this book for me.

CHAPTER ONE

Spanning the Years

We operate on different planes, you and I.
Sometimes they seem miles away from each other.
These are the times that tear me apart—
  when the words just won't fit the thought,
  and there are no ears to hear.
And then there are the times
  we soar together, perfect complements.

When you think of change you also might think of the word"scary." Change *is* scary. Change means venturing into the unknown—to, as any good "Trekkie" knows, "boldly go where no one has gone before."

Change means a new way of thinking about the patterns of life handed down from generation to generation. Change means taking risks; behaving differently from how you have behaved in the past. This is where the scary part comes in.

However, as Heraclitus said, "It is in changing that things find purpose." And in his inaugural address, President Bill Clinton asked all of us to "make change your friend." One of the things that make human beings distinct from other life forms is the ability to evaluate, to see patterns, and to make changes. To do so often requires courage.

Over and over you may have asked yourself, "What am I doing wrong? What makes every relationship I have go sour and never end in commitment? Why can't I find the special someone that everyone else seems to have?"

You may be trapped by same limiting ideas. "If only I were younger ... If only I were older ..." "If only I could have, if only I would have." So you become caught in a series of "what if" and "if only" questions. You lapse into the hypnotic state of a daydreamer, only seeing relationships work if they remain fantasy. God forbid that fantasy could become fact!

The bad news is that the perfect prince or princess does not exist except in fairy tales. Furthermore, life is not a fairytale. But the good news is that we can "create," if you will, the perfect partner. How, you are no doubt asking, can this be done?

Let's say a person shows up in your life. Maybe this relationship exists merely on the fringes of your life, but is nevertheless a sudden force of hurricane proportion—and you aren't prepared for such a relationship. Perhaps you are an older woman and a younger, maybe a much younger, man sweeps into your life, challenging all the old taboos and "can't dos" and "no-nos" that have been such a basic part of your development. Or perhaps you are an older man and a younger, maybe a much younger, woman appears on the threshhold of your life, and suddenly you're thrown into overdrive with all the old tongue-wagging statements and limitations that society has formed about this sort of relationship.

This dilemma robs you of sleep, of work, of food, of even dignity, because you believe that this is only something that you read about and that happens to other people, but never, never to you!

But let's say it has happened. Suddenly you are faced with some very real questions, the foremost of which is, "What about the difference in our ages?" Two issues are at hand here.

2

"What will my friends (or family, or other people) think," and, "How much do I care what they think?"

While this book is specifically about age different relationships, these issues can apply to any "different" relationship—race different, culture different, religion different, or any other different relationships.

You might as well confront yourself with these questions first, because everyone else is soon going to be confronting you when you dare to mention that you are seeing so-and-so, and everyone knows so-and-so is older or younger than you.

Following are some of the questions you can ask yourself as a preparatory measure. Although this is not a "pass/fail" test and no one is going to grade your answers, be honest. An honest approach will make a difference as you progress through this book. If you kid yourself, or if you cheat on your answers to hear what you want to hear, then you will have gained nothing for your trouble.

1. *How many years are there between us?*
2. *What is the apparent emotional year span?*
3. *Will I be embarrassed because he/she looks older/younger than me?*
4. *What is attracting me to this person?*
5. *What do we have in common?*
6. *What do we not have in common?*
7. *What appears to be attracting this person to me?*
8. *Has this person ever been in an age different relationship before?*
9. *What's making this person available now in my life?*
10. *If I were with this person, could we "take the heat?"*
11. *What am I up to in life; what do I think I'm here to do?*
12. *Can this person help me do what I think I'm here to do or not do?*

These questions provide a good beginning for you to

examine whether you are willing to span the years, years that might cover one, two, or even three decades. You will get a "jump start" on the process if you consider adding questions of your own. Go ahead and use the same approach to list making you might use if you were shopping for a new car, or comparing appliances, clothing, or schools. On one side of your paper write "pro," and on the other side write "con."

You may notice there may be many more items on the "con" side of the list when you first start putting it together. Don't be frightened. The reason the negatives will seem to outweigh the positives is that convention and resistance are getting in the way. "Convention" can be defined as the way in which you have performed or acted before, your socialization, the total impact of your upbringing. In this context, resistance means the fear of perceiving yourself in a new and different way as a member of a relationship. These pieces of your background are who you are, so challenging these pieces, even looking at them, can be frightening. Meeting these challenges, however, is also the prelude to changing the pattern of your life.

Now comes the hard part. If there is to be a bridge built spanning the years between the two of you, you must start doing part of the building. We say "part of the building" because, after all, the other part of the building will have to come from your partner's efforts.

Accepting responsibility for building the relationship is an extremely important concept. In any relationship, forming identity as a couple is a function of commitment. Challenging norms is a task that is always difficult. To challenge such norms as an age different couple requires an uncommon sense of unity.

Probably the single overriding question that will set the tone for the answers to any of the questions, on our list or yours, is, "How much of an effect on my life will this age difference make?" It is likely that you are not interested in starting this relationship if it is only going to be short-term. Maybe you think the attraction will pass, that it is just a fleeting and overwhelming feeling you have for each other, a physical need and superficial chemistry more than something truly substantial.

No relationship has much of a chance for success unless both parties agree it is leading to some sense of permanence. This does not necessarily mean marriage, but it does mean that old "C" word again: commitment.

Let's talk about that word, "commitment." It may not matter whether marriage is the immediate or the ultimate goal. We know what matters is that two people have sought each other and, finding each other, are willing to look at a monogamous relationship.

A good rule of thumb is this: if a difference in age is used as an excuse by either of you to refrain from commitment, then sooner or later you will use that excuse again to justify other failings in the relationship, and the relationship will ultimately not survive.

Commitment is difficult, and not difficult because of differences in ages. Commitment is difficult because, in any situation, you are saying you will be there no matter what, that you will do what needs to be done, and that you will do everything you can to make the relationship work. Unfortunately, the requirements of such a committed association seldom are fully specified before the commitment is made. This, then, is the risk inherent in commitment.

A difference in ages between partners can challenge commitment, so you must get beyond the age difference right at the very beginning. This difference must not be like a wart on the end of a person's nose which prevents you from detecting their beauty.

Remember a relationship, your relationship, is like any

other living, breathing organism. It requires nurturing and support, encouragement and feeding. More than anything else, it requires a commitment that this is the way you both want to spend your time together for the forseeable future.

Each of you is unique. Together you may become something greater than each of you separately. You have a presence and an identity as a couple beyond your separate identities. Your relationship lives as an entity, and it requires no less attention than you do as an individual.

The avoidance of the "C" word, particularly among men, has become the hue and cry of many of the eligible females in the country today. However, lack of willingness to make a commitment may no longer be unique to men. Rather, such reluctance to commit may be a function of our times. Both men and women no longer expect to keep the same job for very long. In fact, staying in the same job for more than five years can be a career killer. We may have come to identify business and the economy as culprits in this change. Have you considered how these factors may have affected your feelings about commitment in your personal relationship?

"What the hell is wrong with him/her that he/she can't make a commitment?" is a common cry heard in therapists' offices across America. That cry can become a plaintive wail and be turned inward. It becomes, "What the hell is wrong with *me* that he/she doesn't want to make a commitment?"

Well, there are some theories about what reasons we may not nurture the "C" word today as it has been nurtured in the past. Many of the eligible young urban professionals, the "yuppies," aren't so young anymore, but are still eligible. The problem is, they are products of an era during which many of them have seen their parents' long-term marriages end in divorce, and sometimes have witnessed multiple divorces.

The marriages made in the 60's have had a difficult time surviving into the 90's. The result is that the offspring of such

6

broken marriages simply don't trust the process anymore. For them, commitment isn't valued in the way it might have been valued in decades past.

However, fear of the "C" word doesn't hold as much power over a relationship in which there is an age difference. When two age different people first get together, they are already investigating the possibility of change and, therefore, the frightening aspects of commitment have already been confronted to some extent. However, a fear of commitment in these relationships may rear its ugly head for other reasons. Perhaps you have been divorced, were abandoned, or have been disappointed before in a relationship. Nevertheless, in a relationship involving an age difference, possibilities for new approaches arise.

Often, individuals in such relationships don't have any "old tapes" playing about the lack of success of age different relationships, because neither themselves nor their parents have been involved in such an arrangement before. That's the good news. There aren't any old bad experiences about an age different relationship to clutter up their thinking.

The bad news is this: commitment, or a lack of commitment, might still be the hook on which either party wants to hang their hat if this relationship doesn't work out.

When a couple, any couple, begins putting energy into whether or not they should even be a couple, then the relationship is in trouble. In age different relationships, the decision to be a couple is the first hurdle. After that hurdle is passed, commitment can be an open field on which to run.

The energy each of you applies to the relationship can span the difference in your years. It is this energy, dedicated to discovering the new and wonderful aspects of the life and time of the other, that will be the basis of the bridge across those years.

The older person can bring a sense of "having been there

and survived" to the younger one. The younger party can bring a definite sense of "let's try it this way and see what happens," a sense of adventure and possibilities.

So you see, there is a payoff for both of you not tied into or dominated by old tapes. Both of you will have an obligation to keep a very open mind and not dismiss the other's point of view as one that has come from outmoded thinking or the naivete of youth.

Thus, step by step, you span the years between you, no matter how many they may be. One of you will definitely bring experience, but this can also quickly turn into a terrible weapon we call "parenting." Parenting is a dastardly attitude which can quickly remind the younger party of the reason they left home in the first place. Equally dangerous is the chance the younger party may fall into the role of child.

The younger person can often find a reason that situations should be handled their way, because the older method "obviously" won't work anymore. The older person can tend to assert that experience knows best. Age different relationships do not hold a premium on these behaviors; they simply make falling into them a little easier.

See how much fun all this can be? Age different relationships offer great lessons in tolerance for the other person's point of view. These lessons are based on a real effort to bridge the age difference between you, rather than defending a point of view simply because that's the way you've always done it.

A basic tool for help in spanning the years is to acknowledge that you each can learn something from the other. Maybe this may sound like a turn-off for you if learning is not your interest, but be assured that this kind of learning is different. For instance, if you are the younger partner, how often have you had the opportunity to engage in a historical perspective of a time in which you did not actively live?

The popular television program, *Quantum Leap*, deals

with just such fantasy, catapulting its hero back through various time warps to let the audience relive some piece of history while entertaining some modern methods of problem resolution along the way. The great surge in popularity for classic films such as *Casablanca* and *Citizen Kane* constantly point to the idea that people from one generation always have a basic eagerness to learn from another generation.

On the other hand, an older partner can learn to appreciate new things from a younger partner; music that may have seemed like "loud noise" before an introduction to the pop culture can become a source of enjoyment, as can an understanding of what makes it very special to the younger party. The thrill of a live symphony orchestra, something that may have been disregarded as "long hair" by a younger partner, can take on a new and fresh vibrance for both parties as the older partner patiently leads the younger one into that world—not parentally, but with an air of excitement at sharing something you love with a special person in your life.

Each learning experience between the two of you is like receiving another volume in the library of life. The older partner has an opportunity to be introduced to the culture of a new generation, and the younger one has the chance to be ushered firsthand into a world of another time or decade.

We remember the particular thrill that was ours at sharing our first concert together, standing and clapping and beating our hands in tempo to the rock sounds filling the night air at Red Rocks Amphitheatre. The experience was exhilarating for two reasons: Cyn was capturing some music live and direct from one of her culture's heroines, and Jack was sharing an excitement that was contagious. There were no gaps in years that night, only the opportunity to understand what was making it so special for Cyn and also what was making it so special for Jack. He would never have gone without her, and thus would have missed what made this concert so great, and what made the star so popular with Cyn's age group.

Cyn had an opportunity to find out that some of the work performed wasn't so new after all, but was updated and reorchestrated from some popular works of another era, one she had never experienced. Together, then, we bridged our own age difference in two ways: music and learning. We felt the magic long after the last chords from the amplified guitar died away.

Spanning the years between you is a fun project, not a chore, and should be a never-ending experiment in blending what is known with what is unknown. Therein lies much of the recipe for success in an age different relationship. Each day and night can be a surprise package of experiences, some from the present and some from the past. All these experiences blend to make your time together a kaleidoscope of vivid color and everchanging patterns in your relationship.

10

CHAPTER TWO

Finances: Your Checkbook or Mine?

Put your fear on a leash and watch it dance
  around you—
  sometimes leading, sometimes following.
When it lays down to rest occasionally, pat it on
  the head
  and acknowledge it's there with you.
Just always remember: you are holding the leash.

You don't have to be in an age different relationship to have anxiety about the subject of money. The way we handle money, or don't handle money, is a product of old tapes we have brought forward from many different sources. These old tapes are created in part by the ways our parents raised us. Issues we handled with family members, with our former partners, and with others contribute to old tapes as well.

Think about your own childhood. Did you receive an allowance? Were you paid to do certain chores around your house? Or were you not paid because your parents believed that every family member should contribute their fair share to the household maintenance as part of their responsibility to the family? Did your parents fight over money issues?

Did you work while in junior high or high school? Maybe you went to work even earlier. One woman we interviewed has vivid recollections of working at the age of six in the family business.

Think about your past relationships. What were they like regarding finances? Then answer these next questions, as honestly as you can.

1. *Did I have my own money as a child? As a teenager? As a partner in a previous relationship?*
2. *Did I contribute to the general fund of my family's household?*
3. *Did I think I contributed more than my fair share to the family household? To the household I shared with a former partner, or to one I presently share?*
4. *Did we fight or argue frequently about money in my family? Did/do my partner and I have such fights often?*
5. *Did/do I bring money of my own into the relationship?*
6. *Did/do I hide my money from my mate?*
7. *If I got a raise, or otherwise increased my personal wealth, did I share the news with my mate?*
8. *Did/do I maintain savings separately from my mate?*
9. *Is it frightening for me to think of being financially dependent on my mate?*
10. *Is it frightening to imagine my mate being financially dependent on me?*

We'll bet you could read these ten questions and add ten or twenty more of your own around the issue of finances. Money is one of the major issues contributing to difficult times between partners in a relationship. We can share many, many personal concerns with the one special person in our lives, but not necessarily our finances.

We can wear each other's Jockey shorts if they are accidently mixed up in the laundry and we happen to wear the same size. We can share deodorant or a toothbrush during a trip if one forgets his or her own. We can share sweaters, tee-shirts, crew socks, automobiles, bicycles, golf clubs (true, the last three can be touchy), and sack lunches. You name it, it's not much of a problem to share, even when it's one of our most intimate possessions. Except, perhaps, our money.

We as individuals are created, to a great degree, by our society, and we often identify ourselves by our careers. Many of us are trying to change that identification; nevertheless, such has been our tendency during the '80s and '90s. "What do you do?" we ask when we first meet someone. Then we evaluate the social respectability of that person's response based on our extensive knowledge of income levels and prestige of different job titles.

In age different relationships, another major element factors into this sizing up process. One of you has made, spent, and saved money longer than the other. Possibly you do not have, and may never have, equivalent incomes.

However, performing a function longer does not necessarily mean performing it better. Living and working on a lesser income, especially as a single parent, may develop qualities of money management one might not learn otherwise. In addition, people do have different strengths and weaknesses. A "left-brained" person may have less experience, but more analytical ability. A "right-brained" person may be more creative, but less able to manage money. The point is, age is not the criterion on which to evaluate money management skills. Ability, socialization, and previous experience all contribute to such an ability.

There is another potential problem. At some point, one of you will begin to lose the ability to earn as much money as you do now, perhaps because of a forced or voluntary retirement.

13

One of you may soon exist on a fixed income. There is also the possibility that the older partner may develop some infirmity which requires special care.

A very difficult issue is, therefore, facing the possibility that in the future one of you may have to live with an infirm person. However, consider that even if you are the younger partner, how do you know that person may not be you? Automobile and other accidents, serious illnesses, or chronic health conditions occur that could, God forbid, mean the younger partner might be the one needing attention. Life is a gamble. Age may have nothing to do with which partner, in an age different relationship, might end up being more dependent on the other.

In an age different relationship, perhaps more than in any other relationship, acknowledgement of social influence is extremely important. The older partner, especially if male, may have been raised to think the man should handle the finances of the family. Or, an older woman who has been raised with the same value may expect her younger mate to be responsible for finances. A person of a younger generation may say those values are no longer valid, yet we still often question whether we have completely escaped the influence of those older values. In an age different relationship, these values may simply be more obvious. We have the power, however, to recognize and overcome them.

Possibly you lived alone for several years. You learned to repair your own plumbing, cook your own meals, and manage your own finances. Maybe you raised, or are raising, children as a single parent. Can there be a more challenging experience, both emotionally and financially, than that? An older man might find his younger mate's independence frustrating if he was raised to believe women are incapable of taking care of themselves. An older woman might find her younger mate's more casual attitude toward spending time and money with friends threatening. The combinations are endless, but the challenge is real.

Those of you who have been around the block once or twice, who are whole and secure and looking for someone with those same qualities, will find some options in these pages to achieve that goal. Once you've found that person, the question remaining is, "What should we do now to make finances a workable part of our age different relationship, rather than a battleground?"

Let's review our previous list of ten questions and explore them a little more deeply. We may see some possible solutions.

1. Did I have my own money as a child? As a teenager? As a partner in a previous relationship?

Of course you did. At least in the more recent past you had some money, even if only what you allowed yourself from your last paycheck. Or you had some savings, a stash of ready cash for the little everyday emergencies that arise. You also might have come into this relationship with considerable personal finances: CD's, stocks, bonds, annuities, inheritances, trust funds, bonuses, and the like. You might have been in the big bucks without the help of the mate with whom you are now sharing a relationship.

For whatever reason, you may be wary of allowing someone else to control your funds. You may have heard a barrage of questions, unsolicited advice, maybe even incrimination, about your control over your own money. Most prenuptial agreements exist primarily to protect the existing funds, art treasures, personal jewelry, furniture, and other more valuable assets one partner might bring to the relationship.

We agree in our opinion that prenuptial agreements can be a setup for failure, that the necessity for such an agreement assumes the relationship will fail. We also understand some circumstances indicate such an agreement may be necessary. If you are concerned, make arrangements on your own through trust funds, wills, or other instruments as advised by your legal and/or financial counselor. Otherwise, you are sabotaging the commitment of the relationship. We suggest you be straightforward about your arrangements from the beginning.

We seriously doubt that 62-year-old P.L.O. chairman Yasser Arafat came into his recent marriage with his 28-year-old former secretary, Suha Tawir, as a poor man. We also would be surprised if they did not have some kind of agreement stating Arafat will not transfer all his wealth to Ms. Tawir just because she is now his wife.

Another absurdity would be to believe the very successful lawyer, 38-year-old Bunny Bread heiress Victoria Reggie, would want to share her fortune with her new husband, 60-year-old Senator Ted Kennedy, although he himself is not exactly listed among the poor in America. Reggie lived in a $725,000 brick colonial home in Washington, D.C., managed a summer home in Nantucket, put both her young children through private schools. A partner in a very successful law firm, Victoria Reggie has obviously "brought something to the table" financially in her marriage to Kennedy. Thinking she would suddenly turn over control of her money to her new husband would be ridiculous, as would thinking the Senator would have his new wife become the controlling partner of his holdings.

So here you are with some money of your own. Now, you begin to experience your first taste of a potential problem if your age different mate cannot match your resources. Your mate may be envious of what you have already saved or accrued. This is a dilemma, but certainly a dilemma that you can resolve.

When one couple we spoke with, Ed and Bev, set up housekeeping, Ed owned the house. Bev had been paying a

16

certain amount for rent for her apartment. She was, however, operating on a very tight budget with no financial support from any source other than her job.

Expecting Bev suddenly to pick up exactly half the combined household expenses was unrealistic. What she did do was to pay the same amount of money to Ed she had paid for apartment rent. In that way, she felt she was contributing to the household, since Ed used that money to help with the mortgage.

Still, the house was Ed's house. Even without a prenuptial agreement, Bev really didn't have any equity or other tangible result of her monthly contribution. They resolved the problem when Ed filed a quitclaim deed on the property, transferring half of the ownership of the house and property to his wife. Bev now feels she is an equal partner in the venture, although she cannot match exactly one half of the mortgage demands.

In return, Bev owned some insurance policies, which she changed to make Ed the primary beneficiary. Although the chances of Bev dying before Ed are remote, this change was her way of bringing something to the marriage she could afford. This contribution was an expression of her desire to be an equal partner within the limitations of her income. If some tragedy does befall Bev, her insurance policies will make up for the income Ed could no longer expect to receive from her.

We are not suggesting there are no rough spots in dealing with money issues in any relationship, let alone age different relationships. We merely suggest that differences in time spent developing careers, family responsibilities, and other factors may contribute to the challenges faced by age different couples. Bev, for example, was always financially independent as a result of her family upbringing. Ed was a very generous person, and felt it was his responsibility to support his wife and family. Each had to change some old tapes to live comfortably, without conflict, with the other. Time, patience, and a continuous commitment to understanding and hearing the other's point of view made all the difference.

If you have your own money, we suggest you keep it, or find an equitable give-and- take situation you both can live with. Let's move on to the second question.

2. Did I contribute to the general fund of my family's household?

In your previous relationship, or relationships, what was the ratio of financial contribution from each partner? If the relationship was one in which both of you were about the same age and earning about the same amount of money, then you might have pooled all your funds, writing out of just one checkbook. However, remember women are still paid about 56 cents on the dollar men earn for the same work. It is unlikely, therefore, that you were both earning the same amount. In fact, if you were the male, you might have been bringing in more income, no matter how much younger you were. Of course, this is not always true, but the point is that most partnerships, especially monogamous relationships, probably do not have equal financial resources coming from each party.

Elena had a first marriage to a man who was fanatical about watching every penny spent, though the two of them had a handsome income. Following her divorce, Elena became involved in a relationship with an older man who treated her as if she wanted to take advantage of him financially. Understand that Elena had always worked, had continually worked throughout both relationships. She had even supported her first husband when he was fired from his job. She had always made a decent, if not excessive, income on her own. Nevertheless, after two such relationships, patterned very much like her relationship with her father, Elena was understandably reluctant in her latest, also age different, relationship to relinquish control of her income or to do anything less than contribute her fair share to the household expenses.

One problem in Elena's latest relationship with Josh was that she was inflexible and defensive about the issue of money and financial contribution. Modeling her mother's behavior, Elena concealed purchases—even necessary day-to-day purchases—from Josh for fear of he would criticize her spending habits. If Josh made any comment about his contribution versus hers, Elena perceived it as an attack on her ability or willingness to contribute equitably. Josh, as her older mate, wanted to pool resources, as he was raised to consider this normal. Elena, however, remained adamant that they handle their finances separately.

Josh and Elena eventually developed a solution. They opened three accounts: hers, his, and a joint account to which each contributed for household expenses. We will go into the details of this arrangement later in this chapter.

What's important for you to decide is whether your arrangement in a previous relationship worked for you as you contributed to the household fund. Or were there expenditures or income you did not want to disclose to your partner?

In an age different relationship, one major consideration is which partner has the greater ability to contribute to the general fund. Thus, we move to the next question.

3. Did I think I contributed more than my fair share to the family household? To the household I shared with a former partner, or to one I presently share?

If you did think you contributed more, also ask yourself, "How did that make me feel?" Your feelings about your answers to these questions are cornerstones on which to develop your ability to communicate with your partner. If you were putting more into the money pot than your partner, did you feel resentful? Angry? Abused? All of the above? Maybe. You may, therefore, have an understandable reluctance to be in a relationship in which you once again are responsible for carrying most of the financial load.

Now some age different factors really begin to show up. If you are an older man, the chances are that your background, your upbringing, your very work ethic, have caused you to believe the male partner's responsibility is to be the breadwinner. We know this is pretty antiquated thinking for the 1990s, as more females are advancing their professional lives and are able to assume responsibility for a larger share of the financial pie. But the reality is that it still exists.

What may be part of an older man's thoughts is the impact on his ego if his younger partner is carrying more of the financial burden. This can become a major area of dispute. He might consider her ability to contribute more as an attack on his manhood than as a desire to share her earnings as an equal partner.

Marian is 32, and has just completed medical school and her internship. She is now ready for a residency, which she is seeking as we write this book. Michael is a construction foreman, a former home builder whose company went bankrupt when the home building industry took a nosedive. Michael makes very good money, and plans to reopen his own business if times get better and he sees the market for his custom-built homes improve.

Marian and Michael have been struggling with Marian's education and the enormous cost of her schooling, for which she has taken out student loans. Soon those loans will require repayment. Michael feels he has contributed a hell of a lot more to their finances than his wife. At age 52, he is beginning to harass Marian about "getting into practice and earning the big bucks."

When we talked with Marian and Michael, Marian was about to tell Michael that she was thinking of going into research for a teaching hospital rather than pursue a private practice. She has received several positive responses for her proposed services, and following her residency was planning to interview for at least two positions.

Michael shared, "Hell, I put in a ton of money for her education and her student loans, thinking she would be able to help me get my business going again. Frankly, I feel I was used!"

Marian countered with, "Michael thinks you just finish your residency, hang out your shingle, and start taking in the dough. But it doesn't work that way. My malpractice insurance would absolutely put us back into bankruptcy again. There's no way I can afford that. If I go to work for a large health care facility, then I can't contribute the way I want to. And I'm the one who has invested in these gruelling years to become a doctor!"

Michael is obviously suffering from what we describe as "old tape rerun." Again, our definition of "old tape" is the values with which your parents raised you, the accepted social values of the time during which you developed, and the experiences that may have strongly affected you as an adult.

Michael was not focusing on Marian's contribution to the relationship—the happiness, the common interests, the sexual fulfillment, and the other elements Michael told us attracted him to his younger second wife. Rather, he concentrated on his old tapes from the past, enforcing them with his stereotyped beliefs about doctors and their earning power.

Michael's old tapes might have destroyed this relationship eventually. However, Michael and Marian had one thing going for them. They had discovered and developed the ability to discuss issues and to listen to each other's point of

21

view. They communicate, and that ability will help them through this crisis.

Michael must let go of his old tapes and start playing the new ones Marian is helping him create, so he will not let resentment about whose contribution is greater wreck their relationship.

> 4. *Did we fight or argue frequently about money in my family? Did/do my partner and I have such fights often?*

Sure you did. Doesn't almost everyone? Maybe you still argue about money. Well, we're here to tell you such argument is senseless. Of course, that doesn't stop us from arguing just the same.

If we were to say we never argue about money, you'd probably reply with a sarcastic "Yeah, right." We do argue over money. We tried to think of any couple we know that doesn't occasionally (maybe often) argue over money. We couldn't.

Although such arguments are common, the area of finances may be one in which your age difference could work against you. How? When you begin fighting, arguing, and bickering about money—as most all couples do—the older partner in an age different relationship may begin to become parental. Such a situation is disastrous, but it does happen. We see such relationships occur with work relationships, with age similar relationships, and in other relationships. This behavior is, however, especially harmful to age different relationships.

If you remember your old paperback book about interpersonal relationships, *Transactional Analysis*, you may recognize a few of the behaviors we will describe. Our reason for raising this issue of parental behavior is because, especially in an age different relationship, one of the partners (usually but not always the older partner) may begin to act in a parental mode when an argument about money is in progress. While it can be disastrous in effect, this situation does often happen.

As soon as the younger person hears the older person speaking in a parental mode, that younger person may become increasingly resentful of that manner. That younger person may then begin responding from the "child aspect" of their psyche. We see here, then, a no-win situation. Rather than recreate a fight over your allowance with your mother or father, confront your current mate with the nature of their behavior. Please, look for solutions to your problems, rather than merely attempting to wrongly identify the source of the problems as being an immature or inflexible attitude on the part of your partner.

You might try a tool we use to resolve these kinds of problems. We ask, individually, "What is the real issue here, and what do we need to do to get beyond it?" Our focus is on the money problem itself, and what exactly each of us needs to do to resolve the problem.

For example, let's say your older partner, male or female, is adamant your finances must be pooled. You don't agree this is the appropriate way to manage your finances. Maybe you were burned before by a previous partner. Or, as some women have experienced, perhaps your credit rating suffered because of a divorce. But you truly want to understand your partner's point of view. You are committed to the relationship, and you are certain that understanding your partner's position is critical to improving the relationship.

Discussions involving disagreement or conflict with an age different partner are inevitable. Some of those discussions may involve age-related issues. A tool one of your authors learned could make those discussions fruitful in business is also applicable to relationships. It is a way to derive the root causes of problems.

Before engaging in the discussion, ask yourself, "What is this problem?" Then, "What caused the problem?" And then, "What problem caused that problem?" Repeat this question five times, or even more if the problem is a deep issue. Until you arrive at the root of the major issue causing the problem, whatever it is, you will never resolve it. You will simply continue to apply bandages to the symptoms.

The second tool works so well it can be uncomfortable. It is called the "Ten-Minute Drill." Jack wrote about this technique in his first book, and it is very effective. Once you have asked yourself, "And what caused that problem?" at least five times, it may be time for a ten-minute drill with your partner.

The rules for a ten-minute drill are: Whoever has a specific issue to raise goes first. That partner has ten minutes to speak. You, as the speaker, must use "I" statements only, such as "I feel hurt, angry," whatever. Use a timer. Turn off the answering machine to your phone, or anything else which could distract you. (Put the kids, the dogs, and the cats outside.) The other partner may not interrupt during your turn, nor may you during theirs; doing so is a foul (you can determine your own penalties). During a ten-minute drill, you are there for your partner. You can respond, but only during your turn.

The ten-minute drill can be difficult because you must listen without defending your position until your turn. It can also be one of the most effective communication techniques for any type of relationship. We cannot recall a time in any personal or professional relationship the ten-minute drill has not been effective, assuming the rules were followed.

Age different couples may have a tendency to start hurling incriminations at each other based on life experience rather than focus on what they can change in their relationship to make the money problems go away. We have found it helpful to make sure we are talking about a specific issue, not

24

about money in general. In this way, we arrive at solutions to problems much more quickly, and without the parental issues. Remember, for every parental attack, there will be a child counterattack.

5. Did/do I bring money of my own into the relationship?

We've already touched on this subject, but something helpful to remember about this issue is that you should not allow yourself to be persuaded to "divvy up" finances and make them all even. After all, you are different ages in this relationship to start with. If you are bringing less money into the relationship, you want your partner to know you are not looking for a free ride, and if you have larger savings and/or income, you don't want to compromise your partner's independence.

If you had money of your own, then keep it, or find some reasonable trade-off. What is important is to adopt an attitude of, "We are willing to do whatever it takes to make our relationship work." Some couples can loan money back and forth. Such a procedure works for us. When Cyn had her savings fund built up, Jack borrowed from it temporarily. When he repaid it, Cyn used it for tuition, augmenting her student loans.

When the time came to repay the student loans, Jack used his money to help get Cyn through the rough times. This is how any relationship should work. The important point here is to recognize that Cynthia could maintain her savings account and not have it raided once the need for its temporary use was fulfilled.

6. Did/do I hide my money from my mate?

If your answer to this question was "Yes," you had or have a basic element of trust missing from your relationship. However, if you are still hiding money from your current partner, then you need to ask yourself what else you may be hiding.

An age different relationship must have a solid foundation of trust between partners. If you are going to worry about trusting your younger mate, or worry about what your older mate might be doing without telling you, then you are in trouble from the beginning.

There should be no hiding of funds, no hiding of anything. If there is no honesty between an age different couple, then the relationship will eventually crumble. You may already be fighting enough external forces without the internal force of mistrust pulling at you. External forces can be overcome, but suspicion at the heart of a relationship must be quickly removed or the relationship has no hope of survival.

7. If I got a raise, or otherwise increased my personal wealth, did I share the news with my mate?

We hope so. We hope the envy and mistrust factors would not be so strong that you would feel the need to hide a piece of important financial information. However, we have heard the story over and over.

"I wouldn't tell Carla if I got a raise. She's already spent my next ten raises!" said Tony, a younger man living with an older woman.

Carla responded with, "He thinks I spend all this money on myself. But I don't. When he can't make his child support payment in full, I come up with the balance so his kids won't suffer." They both commented that they don't "talk about money a lot," because such discussions get them in trouble.

This is a case in which Tony's receiving a raise is not really the issue. This couple's communication is so off the mark they are simply using money as an issue. What they need to be working on is the sense of responsibility that is missing in their relationship.

Communication about finances is critical, so that neither

26

gaining of additional money nor spending of existing money can be used as weapons against either partner.

8. Did/do I maintain savings separately from my mate?

This is the result of a basic fear of dependence and financial disaster that may exist in any relationship, but does seem to have more of an impact on age different relationships. People who have had bad experiences guard against those same elements in a new relationship. That's basic survival instinct.

One young woman told us she never knew when she would be asked to leave the relationship, so she had a secret savings account that was her "getaway money." Her new age different relationship still was not strong enough in her eyes to force her to come clean with her new husband about her secret savings.

Francie simply was not completely convinced that her adoring husband, 15 years her senior, wouldn't act like other men she had known and ask her to pack her things and leave someday. So Francie kept her secret savings. We promised to keep her secret from her husband, Jeff. However, Jack, ever the therapist, urged Francie to get counseling for herself to raise her self-image so she would not always think of herself as someone men left. Of course, Francie's father had abandoned her, her sister, her brother, and their mother when Francie was 10 years old. Her mistrust of men remaining in her life was well-founded. What would make her new relationship any different?

Francie needed to recognize her age different husband in a different category from "all the others." Jeff had not shown any similar traits whatever to those men in her earlier relationships, yet Francie was sure he would leave. Tragically, she may well be right, but only because hers is a self-fulfilling prophecy. Unless she seeks help around her issue of men

27

leaving her, Francie can have all the secret savings she wants. The relationship will probably fail because she will do something to sabotage Jeff's interest in trying to maintain the relationship, and "prove" her suspicions were correct.

Having a secret account is just a way of saying, "I don't trust you or this relationship." It's okay not to share the amount you have. Maybe you want to use it for gift-giving or for a nice trip for the two of you. However, withholding that you have a secret account is not a good idea.

In an age different relationship, once a secret source of funds is discovered, there may be a tendency for one of the partners to ask, "What else are you not telling me?" The old tape replay of past hurts and grievances may kick in, and then the relationship is in trouble. The key advice we offer is to remember that age different relationships don't need any unnecessary obstacles to impede success. Such relationships may already have to fight against certain outside forces.

Complete honesty between age different partners is, if anything, even more vital than between closer-aged couples. Age different couples often act more as a unified team, operating from an attitude of, "We'll work harder to make this relationship work," than many other couples. This is exactly the right attitude to have and maintain.

9. Is it frightening for me to think of being financially dependent on my mate?
10. Is it frightening to imagine my mate being financially dependent on me?

Of course it may be scary, and that's okay. But you can deal with the fear responsibly if you realize you are not feeling financially dependent (or worried your partner will be dependent on you) because of the age difference! Take a close look at what's really making you feel this way, and then look at what needs to happen for that feeling to go away. You can work through it, and your age difference does not have to be an obstacle.

We've asked you to look at these questions from your financial past in order to answer the question, "What do we do with finances in an age different relationship so the situation is fair and not the basis for World War III?"

A solution we recommend, as mentioned earlier, is that you maintain three accounts. One for each of you, for your own paychecks, your own bonuses, your own income from whatever sources. The third account is a household account. You can even name this account and have checks printed with a name such as "Baker Street Account," or simply "The J. Jones Household Account."

Whatever you name your joint account, it works as follows: Each week, or twice a month, depending on your pay schedules, you each write a check from your personal account to the household account. This figure is a set amount you have both agreed you can handle, and is based on your income and expenditures. You pay only household bills such as mortgage, utilities, insurance, food, maintenance fees, repairs, and garbage collection out of this account.

If you each have car payments, for example, you would pay from your own personal accounts. Other personal items such as clothing, gifts, and toiletries would also be handled separately. Funds for entertainment and vacations can be held in the household account, or you may want to have a separate savings account for those items. And don't worry about the number of accounts. It's worth it to know that finances are on an even keel in a relationship. This is one solution that can really work.

If one of you receives a raise or some other change in income, you can alter the amount you contribute. The beauty of this plan is you still maintain a sense of personal responsibility to yourself with your own checking account, handling your personal bills and spending habits.

You each join in reconciling the household account. You take turns managing the account, writing checks to pay the bills, balancing the account, and making the deposits. We recommend switching quarterly.

Certainly money can be an issue for any couple; we simply have observed an added dimension to this issue for age different couples. For example, John is several years older than his current wife, Elizabeth. For most of his life, John had been wealthy. Unfortunately, his first business failed some years ago. Although he regrouped and rebuilt a new business, he now has little confidence in his ability to deal with money or numbers. John has always considered himself as more a people-oriented and creative person than as a number-cruncher. Furthermore, from the time he was very young until he met Elizabeth, he had constantly been told by people in his life that he could not handle money.

Elizabeth was a certified public accountant, and studied adult learning as a personal interest. She believed John could learn to manage money. She patiently reinforced his confidence in his ability to do so. John resisted learning to balance his checkbook initially, then became frustrated when it didn't balance. But he believed he could change, and Elizabeth believed math anxiety could be overcome at any age.

Today, John not only balances his own checkbook, but Elizabeth's as well. This couple recognized their individual strengths and weaknesses and worked together to use or overcome them as was appropriate.

John helped Elizabeth with several presentations for her work. His creativity and presentation skills were invaluable to her in attaining her professional goals. Elizabeth was shy and reclusive, but also very ambitious, and recognized such skills were important if she were to attain her professional goals. John helped Elizabeth do what she knew she had to do in order to move on in her career.

Their joint efforts resulted in an increase in John's ability to manage money and an increase in Elizabeth's ability to present herself professionally. She received a big promotion and took on a few private clients, thus increasing their joint income. John assumed responsibility for money management, freeing Elizabeth for her work.

John and Elizabeth are an excellent example of how money issues can be overcome through communication and working together. And they did have to work at it; there were problems, fights, and frustration at times. Yet they persisted in believing in each other and in themselves. They focused on strengths and skills and how they could share them, rather than remaining stuck in their own old tapes or buying into each other's old tapes. They learned from each other based on what each brought to the relationship rather than predetermining each partner's contribution based on age. Each grew as an individual, but even more importantly, they grew as a couple through commitment, belief in each other, and their efforts to make the relationship work.

Finances for the age different couple may sometimes be challenging because the older person has had more years to handle money. But no matter how each of you handled money in the past, the two of you will need to explore new ways of handling it in the future. Together.

31

CHAPTER THREE

Sex: A New Look at an Old Subject

your eyes
*   sparkling seductive jewels*
*   you enchant me*
I am lost in You
*   and I love it*

Let's get some misconceptions and some social preconceptions about the subject of sex out of the way. The fact that two age different people are in a relationship does not mean the quantity of sexual encounters automatically increases— or decreases.

People are often surprised to discover the national average for sexual intercourse among healthy, normal Americans is once per week. Try telling that to the twenty-year-old (or even forty or fifty-year-old) person who is upset because he or she is not having sex three, four, or more times per week.

The fact a man in an age different relationship might be older does not automatically mean he is selecting a younger partner because he fears he will not have sex more than once a week if he stays with a same-age female. As we said earlier, a woman's sexual appetite may increase with age. Healthy men and women can enjoy active sexual lives well into their eighties.

We recognize people often automatically assume an older man involved with a younger woman, especially a woman two or three decades younger, is merely "robbing the cradle" or trying to recapture his sexual youth.

To be truthful, there is ample reason the public has felt this way. There are many scandalous articles and stories in our media about such relationships. Many people have difficulty imagining there is much else between such a couple except a desire on the older person's part to keep sexually active. Has Elizabeth Taylor, at sixty-plus, chosen her latest husband in his thirties because she feels her sexuality waning? Do we automatically assume such is the case? Why can't Liz simply be in love?

Sexual drive does, to some degree, diminish as a natural course of the aging process, but we can ask how much of this diminishment is actually due to:

1. Lack of interest
2. No attempt to rekindle excitement
3. No return to the pleasures of premarital encounters and dating
4. No experimentation with techniques not tried before
5. No effort to maintain one's appearance
6. No free and open discussion of the problem(s)
7. Poor physical condition
8. Closed or embedded attitudes
9. An attitude of "It's over"
10. Laziness

Eleanor, for example, had been involved with a younger man and several older men at different times in her life. Sex with the younger man was more frequent and less meaningful than Eleanor really wanted. With some of her older lovers, sex was also less than satisfying. But she says her present mate, Henry, who is also older, is perfect for her.

Eleanor shared her feelings about her previous relationships with us. We devote considerable space to Eleanor because, unlike many of us, she was able to make changes in her life as a result of observing patterns of her own behavior, and do so without another's guidance. We'll hear from Henry in a later chapter.

"With the younger man, sex was a release, not an act of love. With at least two of my older lovers—one ten, one twenty years older—their ability to perform sexually and to satisfy me was not so great. One had developed skills and techniques that, to some degree, compensated for his lack of ability to achieve and maintain an erection.

"Yet my current mate, Henry, who is older by several years, has no problems in any sexual area. I don't need or want sex every night. He cares for me deeply, and I believe that makes a tremendous difference. Commitment to my younger lover, and to my same-age lovers, was secondary to other concerns—whether their careers, other relationships, or whatever the agenda was. My other lovers simply could not care for me deeply, nor did they have the sexual skill of my present mate.

"I've thought about this a lot," Eleanor told us. "I believe my younger lover was a great person, with great potential. But he worked hard and for long hours. He smoked a lot of marijuana and drank a lot of beer when he wasn't working. He was faithful, but conversation with him was very superficial. He wanted sex just about every night, but he wanted to do it and go to sleep. I began to feel the important issue to him was not who I was, but what I could do for him. And I believe he had a core of compassion that may have enabled him to become a much better lover as he aged. I don't know for certain, because I haven't seen him for years. But I think our problems had to do both with the difference in our ages and our upbringings.

"My first husband was close to my age," Eleanor said, laughing. "You can probably tell I've had a few relationships. He had very little interest in sex—it was too messy. He always had reasons not to have sex. He preferred masturbation because it was cleaner, in his opinion. We had sex only once a year, maybe, during our marriage of about five years. He was also mentally and, occasionally, physically abusive.

"When I left that marriage, I became involved with an older man. He was not well mentally, but I didn't know that for several months. In the beginning, he said he found me attractive; he treated me as if I was attractive, and I desperately needed that validation after my first marital experience. It was not until we had been together for several months that his friends began to tell me about his history of physical abuse. In fact, I didn't learn about any of that until after the first time he beat me. I finally found out he had physically abused every woman he had been with.

"That man, despite the other problems we had, was adequate in the sexual department. But he withheld sex, and I believe he did that to punish me. I had shared with him that the lack of sex in my marriage had been a problem for me. I'm somewhat assertive, and I communicate my feelings. If he didn't like my feelings, he withheld sex.

"After I left that relationship, I became involved with several other older men over time. One had no commitment to commitment. I don't even think he knew the definition of the word. Another cheated—sexually—on me, and only eventually told me about it. I knew before he told me, but didn't want to admit it to myself.

"We worked at the same company, and at one time we were both considered for the same promotion. I backed off from competition with him to give him a shot at the job. He did get the promotion, and he shared his success in securing the job with the other woman. He would not have even been in the running for the job if I hadn't rekindled his interest in it. That total lack of recognition of my sacrifice pissed me off far more than what he did with the other woman he was seeing. I'm good; I would have gotten the promotion. I will never make that kind of sacrifice again."

We mentioned Eleanor made some major changes in her life, and they were often prompted by experiences in her relationships.

"I'm an attractive person, I now know," Eleanor says. "But my first husband criticized my weight, which has never been out of the normal range for my height. If anything, I tend to be underweight according to the standard weight charts. One lover I had for a time, also an older man, an artist, told me I had chicken legs—fat thighs and skinny shins. He also said my stomach wasn't as flat as he thought it should be. Even earlier, a boyfriend in grade school told me I had a swayback. I wouldn't walk in front of a full classroom in school for years because of that.

"But you know what? I did something about it. I studied, I read, and I tried to develop my mind and my self-esteem. Later, people began to tell me I was beautiful. Some of them worked with me to develop my beauty. Honestly, I still don't think of myself as beautiful, but I learned to see the effect I can have on people with my appearance. I discovered that if my body allows me to do what I want to do, then it is a good body. It's not perfect, but whose is? Then I looked in the mirror, and that took a lot of courage initially. Those guys were just wrong. I have slim legs, and they are very long, and they look damned good in a short skirt. They are not the legs of a professional dancer, but then I don't—can't—spend eight hours a day on my legs and my stomach and my biceps. I began to realize that my perception of myself was a hell of a lot more important than anyone else's perception of me. And I began to want to be with someone, if there was such a someone, who liked what he saw when he saw me.

"So what, after all of that crap I'd been through, caused me to become involved in another age different relationship? Especially after many of those relationships had not only not worked, but also had been abusive? I learned I could grow. I did grow. I decided what I wanted in a man. And I was able to do it because never once, not during any of what I went through, did I ever consider giving up on what I wanted and came to believe I deserved. I realized, finally, after a great deal of self-examination, that I needed to be me.

"And the only man I could think of who could accept me was going to be an older man. One who didn't need to compete with me. One who appreciated my relative youth. One who would support me in my professional endeavors. One who didn't mind (terribly) that I wanted to do something other than clean house.

"As I said, I'm somewhat experienced in the search for the perfect mate. When I decided I'd rather live alone the rest of my life than go through what I'd been through before, and that I could be happy that way, my life changed. Henry provides all the validation of my attractiveness and sensuality I need. Men my own age did not. In fact, many older *and* younger men I dated did not. It's very simple to me. I'm appreciated now for my appearance, my intellect, and my achievements by the man to whom I'm married—an older man. Still, I wouldn't trade what I've learned from other lovers, or what I have now, for anything."

Of course, some age different couples reinforce stereotyped assumptions because they demonstrate behaviors that simply underscore what the public already thinks. However, these couples are actually more the exception than the rule.

38

Next, we will deal with another relationship founded not on sexual rebirthing, but more on the alternatives we hope this book will reveal.

There is no question that a relationship with a younger partner can increase the frequency of sex. This does not mean, however, that same age couples couldn't duplicate these increases if they discarded the taboos that have bound them past their so-called "eros" years into what they might describe as the "just staying together" or "getting along" or "comfortable years."

Please allow us to clarify. We discuss frequency of sex because many couples consider frequency as equivalent to the quality of the relationship. We do not necessarily support that belief, although we know frequency of sex can be an indicator of the cohesiveness of the relationship. We also know frequent sex can be a way to avoid other important issues in a relationship.

For some couples, and it seems especially for age different couples without young children, the nature and quality of the experience can make all the difference. A relaxing shared bath, preparing a meal together, watching a movie together, snuggling during the movie, and sharing their bodies after (or during) these activities can leave each partner with pleasurable memories and offer anticipation for the next such encounter. That next encounter may be a week or more later.

One couple we know plans this kind of evening at least once a month. They both work long hours and each has many professional obligations. When they can't spend the time such an evening takes, they are not adverse to the colloquial "quickie."

Sometimes sex is a result of that desire for extensive foreplay. Sometimes sex is a sudden and unexpected desire. Sometimes one partner feels vulnerable or threatened by external forces, and making love offers a sense of comfort. Love between committed partners has a depth of understanding and breadth of meaning.

We find the willingness to share needs, moods, and feelings very common among age different couples. It is also more important, in general, than each partner's opinions or expectations of "how it should be." Such a level of communication seems to enhance sexual intimacy and pleasure.

Perhaps, if we may speculate, this phenomenon has to do with the possibility that age different partners choose each other more consciously, with more awareness of the challenges and demands of the relationship. Most of our couples confirm this speculation.

What should occur between age different couples to enable them to express their sexual lives without being called "victims of midlife crises," "cradle robbers," "gold diggers," "sexual huntresses," "young sluts," "homewreckers," or other names society has chosen as negative stereotypes for such pairings?

Expectation plays a very important part in seeing that age different sex occupies its rightful place in the relationship. And dealing with expectation means the couple may have to change attitudes they have held previously. For one such example, let's look at the story of Sandra and Mark.

Sandra, at age 34, was married once before, but had no children. Mark, age 52, was married before for 17 years. He had two children by that marriage, neither living with him. Mark talked about his first flush of excitement at the prospect of sexual involvement with a woman who was 18 years his junior. His expectation was that Sandra probably would want sex at least three times a week, which he thought would be great.

Mark had conveniently forgotten that when he and his first wife were Sandra's age they didn't have sex three times a week. Often ten or more days passed without sex, and they were comfortable with that pattern.

Sandra had a different expectation problem. She assumed Mark would not want, or might not be able, to have sex frequently. They discovered that both of those expectations were way off base.

Mark told us he finally summoned the courage to share his feelings about Sandra's sex drive. More accurately, he shared his thoughts about what he assumed was her sex drive.

"We weren't very far into the conversation," he told us, "when Sandra interrupted with, 'Where did you get the idea I wanted sex three times a week?'"

Expectations. As Sandra and Mark talked, they realized they each needed an attitude adjustment. Mark told her he was perfectly capable of having sex more than once a week, but often it wasn't necessary or important.

Sandra said she and Mark began to realize they were falling into the stereotypical profiles of age different relationships which society had set on their table. He was older and probably couldn't "do it." She was younger and probably "wanted it" more.

"Mark had forgotten the main attraction I had for him was not sex with an older man. I could have all of that I wanted, since I have always been attracted to men older than me. The real driving force for me was here was a man who would listen to me. That was a real turn on after years of feeling I was speaking into a dark, black void."

"Yeah," Mark added. "When we started dating, I had a real fear that I was going to have to 'perform,' you know, and that really made me uptight."

Sandra said, "When we finally did have sex, Mark told me something like, 'My God, it's really okay, isn't it?' We both laughed a lot during our postcoital state that night!"

Looking at just that one example, it's easy to see how

41

sharing sexual expectations can be of paramount importance to the age different couple. After all, such partners are
as much products of their past attitudes as anyone else. We
recommend the sharing of sexual expectations for any couple.
For age different couples, it is a prerequisite.

Expectations, unacknowledged and undiscussed, can
destroy any relationship. Such expectations can also be
threatening if exceeded by one partner. This topic leads us to
a delicate and difficult subject we will discuss often in this
book: change.

Let's return to Eleanor. Eleanor had many relationships.
Yet she never gave up on herself or her ability to change
herself, to grow into someone who could attract and maintain the interest of a man with whom she wanted to be. The
vital point here is she did not make those changes only to
attract such a man. Eleanor's underlying intent was to understand herself and her capabilities. She taught herself to be
happy living alone, and to pursue her own interests for her
own growth and satisfaction. When she met Henry while
pursuing one of her personal interests, she considered his
interest in her a gift, not an expectation.

Common myth suggests that older men are less virile.
Eleanor feels that such a belief is a self-fulfilling prophecy.
"Henry is slower, more skilled, and it's true he usually can't
make love more than once a day if he achieves orgasm. But
he makes me feel so desirable, such a sensual person, that I
wouldn't trade him for ten of the younger lovers I had before."

The secret of their happiness, however, is that Eleanor
and Henry discussed expectations early in their relationship.
Our other couple, Mark and Sandra, learned their sexual
appetites were driven just like any other couple, and that
sexual appetite and sexual prowess do not have to be proven
to justify the relationship.

In an age different relationship, sexual comfort is a key

element. In fact, all aspects of your relationship should feel comfortable to you. If both partners don't feel comfortable, for heaven's sake, don't do it—whether it's sex, buying groceries together, or picking vacation spots as a couple.

As Mark and Sandra discovered, sharing their expectations openly saves a great deal of stress and game playing that can sabotage a relationship from the beginning. Does this mean that Sandra and Mark were sexually active early in their dating? Yes, they were, and they realized the expectations each might harbor, unless discussed, could create a barrier to something that was progressing very well.

Age different partners also find opportunities to teach one another about sex. This may sound ridiculous, but it is true. When you are a decade or more apart in age, the language, the accepted behaviors, the ways you approach sex can be quite different.

Just look at this very simple example. When you were in your teen years, what did the term "making out" mean? Was it:

1. Just kissing?
2. Necking?
3. Petting?
4. Heavy petting?
5. Intercourse?

Now ask what that term meant to your partner. You probably have two entirely different definitions. Now try this exercise with terms which are a little more personal. Think of all the words and expressions you have ever heard for sex acts of any kind, and write them down together.

Not only might the terms or expressions that either of you have never heard before amaze you, but you may also share some terms that are indigenous to the part of the country in which you were raised. At a human sexuality

43

workshop for therapists several years ago, the workshop leader listed more than two hundred and fifty different words or phrases on a large blackboard as the therapists volunteered all they could think of which described some act of sex.

After you've finished your own list, you can reach a better understanding of the influences which have shaped your attitudes and expectations. You can begin to factor in the age difference there might be between you, consider the section of the country from which you came, and identify the back alley slang you learned and your exposure to reading and viewing material. Now you've got a great idea of how much talking you both might want to do before much action takes place!

There is no question that fantasy plays an important role in the sexual aspect of the age different relationship. The very nature of the relationship itself can be a kind of fantasy; a relationship with someone is who older, more experienced, less demanding, less critical. Or, on the other hand, someone younger, more energetic, dynamic, willing to try different things.

Beverly says of her relationship with a younger man, John, "I had never wanted to hear my partner's fantasies before. I felt threatened. I thought they meant he would leave me to find someone closer to his fantasy. With John, though, I feel so completely cherished for who I am that I am not threatened by his fantasies. We act out many of our fantasies together. We observe only two agreements—we do not share fantasies about other real people, only characteristics, and we always play to the fantasies the other creates. We are comfortable enough with each other to know the boundaries.

"I'm fascinated by Japanese culture and the samurai philosophy. John does a wonderful samurai, costume and all. He bathes me, feeds me, and prepares a traditional Japanese

44

tea ceremony.

"I arranged for him to be at a particular nearby hotel bar one weekend. I prepared and packed a complete dinner to serve in the room I had reserved for one night. I wore a wig, a sexy dress, and picked him up in the bar. I left first, but gave him the key to the room and asked him to meet me there. I'm a redhead, but we still joke about the blonde he picked up whenever we stay in that chain of hotels."

An older partner can often bring a sense of security and safety to fantasy. The younger partner may bring a sense of adventure and creativity. Sometimes, however, these roles can be reversed. This is one reason to continue to challenge expectations and social conditioning. If the relationship works, you may each contribute characteristics neither of you might have expected from the other.

There is a wealth of opportunity as you explore love-making with each other, to couple the older partner's experience with the younger's enthusiasm. This enthusiasm may not be bounded by conventions or rules of older generations.

We think of the wonderful, very age different characters, Holling and Shelly, on the television series *Northern Exposure*. Shelly has a devil-may-care, let's-have-at-it attitude. Poor Holling is constantly taken by surprise at her forwardness, her assertiveness, her open and youthful attitude about sexuality.

In the beginning, Holling appeared shocked. ("Stunned" may be a better description.) Soon, however, he realized he was in a relationship which was totally different from anything he had experienced before. That difference, as presented by Shelly, became addictive for Holling. Now we see him very much as a partner in many of the new ideas Shelly presents.

This is another key point for the age different couple. Keeping an open mind, being willing not to automatically reject another's sexual practices from another age, is important in sexually spanning the years of the age difference.

One of our couples, Jennifer and Mitch, talked to us very candidly about their use of photography in their sexual encounters. Jennifer is a professional photographer who does freelance fashion assignments for local advertising agencies. She is the older partner, at 42, in the relationship with Mitch. Mitch, a television producer, recently turned 30.

Jennifer has used a camera for years. She has done many layouts that are exciting, colorful, and provocative. She has also shot a very beautiful portfolio of nudes. Jennifer and Mitch demonstrated no embarrassment or shame as they spoke of nude shots of Jennifer taken in Mexico on some luxurious beach. These photos were taken by a former colleague of hers, a man she knew before becoming Mitch's wife. Both Mitch and Jennifer were fond of these photos, and Mitch was equally enthusiastic about the nude portraits Jennifer had made of him.

"These picture-taking sessions have been an incredible experience for both of us," Mitch said. "Many times we have spent hours costuming ourselves or playing out some character fantasies, which we then photograph."

"We won't share those with you!" Jennifer laughed. "Some things remain very, very private!"

We asked what Mitch had contributed to this venture besides the obvious loan of his body for her camera work.

"Video!" Jennifer blurted with enthusiasm. "Mitch has grown up with television and with a Camcorder as a replacement for an arm, I think."

"Well, Jennifer is damn good with the still photography, but she has never done anything with video. I eat, sleep, and dream video daily in my work. Making videos with Jennifer is very exciting and rewarding for both of us, I think. Don't you, Jen?" he asked.

"Yeah, it is. I would have to say I was turned off in my last relationship by all the X-rated films my boyfriend insisted we watch together. He got turned on watching those movies, and I was really pissed off when he wanted to fool around with me after being turned on by someone else.

"This is really different because it's us," Jennifer continued. "I never realized how exciting it can be for Mitch and I to photograph or videotape each other. It's an extremely intimate thing, and no, we won't show our videos to you, either!"

Jennifer and Mitch represent another example of how each partner can complement the other in an age different relationship. Jennifer, older, an experienced fashion photographer, shares her intimacy on film with her husband. Mitch, in turn, shares his knowledge of the video medium with Jennifer. Thus, both Jennifer and Mitch bridge an age gap and enhance their very warm and apparently exciting sexual relationship. They share gifts with each other born of their own times and experiences.

We asked Jennifer, "Would you, or have you, done this sort of thing with men who were more your own age?"

"I tried it once with a guy I was pretty serious about. In fact, we were on the verge of marrying. But when I was nude, or when he photographed me in various stages of undress, he would make a lot of critical remarks about me.

"He would say things like, 'your legs are not really very good from this angle. You have heavy thighs.' Or, 'let's pad that bra from underneath to make it look like you have some cleavage.' Mitch is always complimentary about how I look. I—"

Mitch interrupted her with, "My God, I think Jen has a fabulous body. I feel lucky she's my wife!"

So there you have it. Jennifer is admired by her younger husband, while in a previous relationship, a man her own age was discontented with her appearance and critical of her. Is it any wonder that Jennifer believes in her age different relationship? Is it any wonder that she appreciates an adoring husband who sees in her mature body and her unquestioned professional talent a woman he can be proud of not only as a wife, but also as an equal in a demanding field?

We asked if Mitch tried these things with the women he was seeing before Jennifer.

"Well, this is an honest interview, right?" Mitch laughed. Jennifer gave him a playful punch in the ribs. "Yeah, I always wanted to make my own X-rated movies, you know, without really getting into some of the scuzzy stuff you can rent. But none of the women I thought might be loose enough— that is, not uptight about morals or anything—felt that good about themselves or their own bodies to make anything happen. Jennifer is very secure about who she is and what she has to offer the world. I think that confidence comes from her age and experience. I gotta tell you, it's refreshing and something I never thought I would have in a relationship, much less in a marriage."

Obviously, every person is attracted to a particular type of body. But as we get older, is it possible we look for other qualities, and blends of qualities, rather than for perfection in any one category?

Another couple, Emma and James, discussed their differences in sexual desire. Emma wants sex more often than James does. James, eight years older, enjoys sex—just less often. We asked if Emma ever felt rejected, or less attractive.

"Rejected? Maybe sometimes. Less attractive, no," Emma answered. "Sex just isn't the basic foundation of our relationship. We laugh a lot, we have a lot of fun, and we do many activities together."

James added, "And we talk about it. We keep that difference from simmering and becoming a problem."

With Laurie and Marc, another couple we interviewed, the reverse of what is commonly expected is the case. Mark, 20 years older, has a more frequent interest in sex than his younger partner. They, too, discuss the issue to keep the difference open and disarmed.

None of the people we have mentioned are sexually dysfunctional. They all simply demonstrate differences in libido not based on age or gender alone, but differences found in any two individuals.

We observed less emphasis on physical appearance in the age different couples with whom we spoke. We saw they put much more emphasis on using their bodies for enjoyment—of sex, sports, and each other—than on satisfying their personal vanity. All the couples we spoke with were attractive and made the most of their individual appearances, so we have no doubt that appearance is somewhat important to them. It simply was not the most important factor keeping these age different couples together.

Therefore, for these couples, fantasy enactment focused on fun and pleasure rather than on the perfect (or not-so-perfect) appearance of their own or their partner's body.

We are not suggesting photographing or videotaping each other during elaborate roleplaying is the only way to enjoy sex in your age different relationship. But such activities represent the willingness to take risks, and being willing to change is vital, once again, to bridging the age gap. Risk and change—in thinking about sex, in having sex, and in discussing sex with your age different partner—can greatly enhance your relationship. The willingness to change can free your thinking and open many new vistas of exploration. Opportunities for pleasure based on love, commitment, communication, and respect for each other and for the quality of your relationship then become clear.

49

CHAPTER FOUR

Children: Yours, Mine, or Ours?

Somewhere along the line the kids
went from dolls and toy cars
to MTV and boogie boxes
One's in college now—she doesn't even know
what she dreams her life will be

This is not about *The Brady Bunch*. Sorry. This isn't even about *Married With Children*. It would be convenient if we could make life into a situation comedy program about relationships with children that would tie up all the loose ends in a funny, tidy manner. We could put a big smile on your face, and you would be ready for next week's laugh-a-minute episode. But we can't do that; as you know, life isn't that simple.

Instead, we are going to look at one of the elements which sometimes contributes to the pitfalls aspect of this book. When we talk to couples who are age different, we always get around to the question of children. We also always get the answer, "It's not easy!"

In this chapter and throughout this book, we use the

words "kids" and "children" interchangably to indicate a parental relationship. Included in our definition are very young children, adult offspring, and all those in between.

The November 1992 issue of *New Woman* magazine included an article titled "The Good Stepfather." This article compared the dilemma of stepparenthood to Shakespeare's *Hamlet*.

"Hamlet," Frank Pittman, M.D., wrote, "is a cautionary tale about a young man and his stepfather. Prince Hamlet comes home from college to find that his father, the old king, has died; his mother, Queen Gertrude, has married his uncle, Claudius; and Claudius has declared himself king. Suspecting that Claudius killed the old king, Hamlet feels torn between loyalty to his dead father and loyalty to his happily married mother—a dilemma that leads to the death of nearly the entire cast.

"As it turns out," Dr. Pittman writes, "Claudius really did murder Hamlet's father, but he also did a few things as a stepfather that would have produced disaster in any family. First, he took advantage of Hamlet's mother; second, he tried to displace Hamlet's father; and third, he strutted around claiming he was king. Stepfathers who do any of those three things are going to make some serious enemies in their new family.

"What's a stepfather to do? A good start is to realize that when he marries a woman with children, he does not automatically become their parent: he must build a relationship with the kids, and this will take time." (Of course, the same advice is true for stepmothers.)

So what are the toughest problems in becoming a stepparent? Several difficulties appear to be fairly standard for this topic:

1. His/her children seem to resent me

2. I don't mean to resent his (her) children or the time spent with them, but sometimes I do
3. I'm not sure what my role is with his (her) children

Most people have other problem areas in addition to these. That's to be expected. Before you begin to deal with any other difficulties, however, you probably will need to deal with the three listed above.

One particularly interesting aspect of the third factor arose when we interviewed couples with an older female partner. As a group, these women complained about their role as "surrogate mother" to their partners' young children. One marriage actually broke up because the woman began to feel this was her only value in the relationship. Whenever her husband was supposed to be supervising his children under the terms of his divorce agreement, he would go off to do the things he liked to do. This left his new wife to play mom to his kids.

While she liked his children well enough, Francis felt that she had already done her child-raising duty with her own children. She had little interest in continuing to play that role for her husband's children.

When Francis tried to talk with Jim about this problem, his answer was, "My kids don't ever get the kind of attention from their real mother that you give them. I think they need that, and I don't see why you can't help me out here!"

"Helping out would have been okay with me," Francis told us. "But to Jim, helping meant that he would pick up his kids and spend fifteen or twenty minutes with them in the car driving back to our house. Then he dumped them on me and went to play golf with his buddies. It got really old in a hurry. Besides, his kids really wanted time with their dad, not time with me."

We asked if they had tried counseling about this matter.

"Jim wouldn't go to counseling. He thought I was making a big deal out of it. He promised to change, to spend more time with them. Truth is," Francis said, "he didn't know how to spend time, quality time that is, with his kids. In his first marriage he had pretty much let his wife do the kid-raising. He concentrated more on hell-raising!"

"Where did you meet?" we asked Francis.

"In a bar. In fact, he was the bartender and absolutely the handsomest man in the place. I fell for him hard, especially after we got together for the first time."

"You mean when you went to bed?" we interrupted.

"That's right. The first time we slept together, I was absolutely hooked. I mean, he was the greatest, gentlest, most tender, yet dynamic man I had ever been with. It was bells, whistles, and skyrockets for both of us!"

In the beginning, the children weren't a problem for Francis and Jim. As they began and solidified their dating relationship, Jim was more anxious to please Francis. She said he was more attentive to his kids, and she became lulled by this.

"When we married, after a fairly short courtship—maybe three months or less—he started dumping the kids on me. I should have realized then he may have been looking for a surrogate mother for them, someone to raise them for him, all along."

"Why wasn't his first wife doing that?" we asked.

"Jim wouldn't talk about it much. He just said that when the kids were with me, he could really tell the difference. He didn't have much good to say about his first wife. She apparently ran around on him, leaving the kids with a babysitter. She would go out and meet other men while he was working six nights a week tending bar."

Francis seemed to ponder what she had just said, and it seemed to us that it was somewhat upsetting to her. Then she continued. "Now that I look back on it, though, I don't know how he could have seen any difference in his kids at all. He was never with us to see the difference."

"Are you willing to try an age different relationship again?" we asked.

"I wouldn't rule out an age different relationship by any means. But I damn sure would not want one with a man who had children who needed raising!"

We also need to address the type of relationship in which the man, who is older, has older children who do not need raising. Is this a pleasure or a pitfall? It can be either one, but in this chapter we are going to offer seven tools for making it a positive factor in a relationship. In fact, these tools can be very helpful whether your stepchildren are kids or adults.

Let's look at these ideas and discuss how to make them work. They are in no particular order of importance:

1. *Be yourself*
2. *Don't try to be a stepparent*
3. *Don't try to deal with the children as a group*
4. *Let the children find their way to you*
5. *Don't try to put together another "little family"*
6. *Don't force yourselves as a couple on the children*
7. *Encourage your partner to spend time alone with his/her children*

You will undoubtedly develop some tools of your own. However, we have used these seven tools ourselves extensively and very successfully. We urge you not only to try them, but also to keep them in mind when it appears you may be failing in this important area of relationships with children, whether young or adult.

Now, let's look at these tools in more detail.

1. Be yourself If you are the person in the relationship who

55

does not have the children, then you have to face it. You are the person on trial. Make no mistake about it; you are the intruder. The best antidote to what could be family poison is simply to be yourself.

After Beth first met one of Bill's daughters, they overheard her say during a telephone conversation with her sister living in another state, "You'll like Beth. She wears red Reboks!"

Beth never tried to present an image other than her genuine self. All through the courting process and the eventual marriage, this remained a steadfast rule.

When we talked to a couple in which the male partner was the outsider to the woman's adult children, we noted that he had worn a tie and sportcoat to our Saturday morning breakfast interview. Jana was more casual; she wore jeans, as we did. Jack asked whether Tim had to go to work directly from breakfast.

"No, no. I just have this meeting for this morning."

Cyn said, "You didn't need to dress up for us. We want you to feel relaxed and comfortable."

Jana provided a clue. "That's just how Tim is. He never wears a tie out to breakfast with just me. I told him to dress like he always does, but no, he couldn't be himself!"

We asked about Tim's relationship with Jana's teenage son and daughter, and learned something about Tim's inability to relax around them as well.

"I think it's okay," Tim told us. "We seem to get along all right."

Jana added, "When Tim and I were dating, my kids were impressed with how casual Tim was. We all seemed to have fun when we were together. Lately, though, Tim seems to feel he has to impress Luke and Sarah with the fact he's a big corporate lawyer."

We learned part of the problem in the relationship was Tim's apparent stuffiness with Jana's kids. He maintained control in the relationship by assuming a very parental stance, not only with her kids, but also, we soon sensed, with Jana as well.

Remember, the ability to be yourself is one of the attributes that attracted you to each other in the first place. Because you are age different, you had many old attitudes to break down with each other. It was and is important for the older partner not to adopt the image of know-it-all. Such an attitude can put down the younger partner on a 24-hour basis. The opposite can also occur. If the younger partner feels insecure about his or her age, he or she may act artificially formal so as to appear "grown up."

Being yourself means being willing to show your vulnerable side. What makes this tool so important is that his or her children will either accept or reject your relationship based on their ability to see the real you. Thus, you need to establish a relationship between you and your partner's children which is genuine from the beginning, so you do not have to correct false impressions later.

2. Don't try to be a stepparent The children of your partner probably have another parent. You, the intruder, have to face the fact that you must not violate their relationship with that parent. But if you have a death wish for your age different relationship, then by all means insist you be treated as stepmom or stepdad.

It's best if your partner's children begin by thinking of you and treating you as mom's or dad's lady or gentleman friend. Later, if there is marriage, it's proper to be introduced to friends of your partner's children like this: "This is my dad, and his wife, Mary." Or, "Stan, you remember my mom, Susan, and this is her husband, Scott Cranston." Encouraging this kind of behavior fosters a healthy respect between you and the children of your partner. It also allows them to continue their

57

individual and collective respect for their own natural mother or father.

Any derogatory banter about the ex-wife or ex-husband is strictly forbidden, and does not become you as the outsider. Nor, we believe, should it even be fostered between the children and their parent who is your mate. Ridiculing or allowing jokes at the expense of the absent partner does not reflect positively on you. You have enough hurdles to clear with the age difference without engaging in destructive ex-mate bashing.

Equally important is for you, if you are a parent, to not speak negatively of your ex-mate in front of the children. Doing so can only cause conflict and confusion for them. In some cases, the children may blame your new mate for your animosity, and this can happen with adult children as well as young ones. Although such a reaction is not necessarily rational, it is human and it does happen.

Marion, one of our interviewees, told us, "I was old enough when my parents divorced to know they weren't happy together. I know they've had some confrontations since then. But one thing I've always appreciated is that during all these years since, neither of them ever said an unkind word about the other in front of my brother and me. And neither have either of their current spouses.

"We're fortunate we never felt we had to take sides or handle nasty comments. Now, as I near forty and my brother is in his mid-thirties, we could probably address the issue. But teenagers, and certainly younger kids, don't need and can't handle that kind of pressure. At least I know I couldn't have, and I was a pretty mature kid."

If children are part of your age different relationship, whether directly or peripherally, think about their position. Refraining from negative remarks about their other parent eases the way to their acceptance of the new mate. It also allows both of you to work toward harmony in your new life, without unnecessary bitterness and resentment.

3. Don't try to deal with the children as a group If there's only one child involved, you can skip this tool and move on to the next. However if your partner has more than one child, you are making a mistake if you try to deal with them as a group. They will outnumber you, outfox you, and outmaneuver you. Worse, you will never get to know them individually, nor will they have a chance to develop individual relationships with you.

Treat them as individuals. Do not make plans with them as a group, and remember it is not necessary for all the children to attend a function you are hosting if there are conflicts. Extend invitations to each of the kids individually, so they know they each have importance in your life.

And when you feel your partner's children are ganging up on you, that's a sure sign you need to follow the old rules of warfare and football. Divide and conquer!

4. Let the children find their way to you This tool is actually an extension of the first and third tools. If your partner's children begin to know the genuine, sincere you, they will know your strengths as well as your weaknesses. One or more of them may seek you out to ask your opinion, or to have you listen, even if what they want to do is complain about their natural parent. In the event they would rather engage in "mate bashing," you must remove yourself from the loop. You do this by saying to the offspring, "That's something you need to take up directly with (insert name of new mate). I'm sure he/she can handle it."

Their problems with relationships, school, careers, and other areas might be shared much more easily with you, the outsider in the relationship, than you imagined. The children will either accept the age difference between you and your

59

partner or reject it altogether, and in so doing, reject you.

If the latter is the case, you won't help the situation by trying to win over the kids. Let them find their way to you. If they need to vent their anger at you, then let them do so, as long as they do not become abusive. When the children eventually understand that you are in this relationship because it is special and rewarding for you and their parent, then they will decide to either find their way to you or to leave you out of their lives. When the children see that you will not abandon ship, that you remain sincere, and that you treat them as individuals with valid opinions, then you will make progress. You cannot force the issue.

5. Don't try to put together another "little family" Face it—it's one of the most natural reactions in the world. You want to please everybody. You want to prove that just because there is an age difference between you doesn't mean you cannot be a family again, right? Wrong. Forget it. For that matter, try not to even think about it.

You have enough of a load to carry facing the challenge of spanning the years between you and your partner without trying to rebuild the Roman Empire. Whatever family existed in you or your partner's "previous lives" (as we refer to past relationships), you are sadly mistaken in your thinking to try to blend a new family circle.

This does not mean you can't have family functions together. You can celebrate holidays, have picnics, throw birthday parties, and so on. But you celebrate as separate entities. The children celebrate with you and your partner as a couple, and then with their other parent or their own partners.

This also does not mean you can't share the traditions you may have brought to the relationship. For example, Cyn's family has a tradition of making a big deal out of Christmas stockings. Jack usually just ran around at the last minute and stuffed the usual apples, oranges, candies, nuts, and maybe a small gift into the stockings hung by the fireplace.

When Jack's kids came to celebrate Christmas Eve, they discovered that Cyn had made elaborate and wonderful Christmas stockings for each of them. His kids were accustomed to their traditional Christmas routine of eating dinner, tearing into their packages, and then hustling off to church together.

Cyn changed that—subtly. Now, everyone takes some time to look through their stockings. There are clever little individually wrapped gifts—a pair of earrings might be lodged among some new scissors or ballpoint pens. Small workshop tools find their way into these stockings, along with handmade notecards or other surprising little items. The underlying message is, "Hey, gang, this is what my family does at Christmas, and I want to share it with you!"

It's funny, but Jack's children now spend time shopping for stocking stuffers. They even bring gift stockings to Christmas Eve, along with their major gifts to share. Cyn did not attempt to put together another "little family," but by sharing a family tradition she has helped to make this new set of relationships workable.

Here's a question to ask yourself relating to family dynamics: Have you given, or do you plan to give, housekeys to the kids? Your answer is probably "no," and why shouldn't it be? For what reason would you do that unless they live with you? The point here is they need to respect your privacy just as much as you respect theirs.

A couple that was very successful financially had an enormous difficulty with this concept, and it was one of the major reasons their relationship had become strained. Here's what happened:

Kenneth, a wealthy industrialist, had two young adult

children. His daughter still lived with her mother, and his son traveled between several west coast cities in which he had branch offices of his car rental business. His business was financed originally by dad, of course.

Kenneth had married his very capable administrative assistant. She was childless and 20 years his junior. She had definite opinions about a number of issues, and her opinions ruffled the two kids. The son and daughter both had been given keys to their father's various residences which he maintained around the country—a summer home, a mountain retreat, a coastal home, and the like.

When the wedding was over and the time seemed right, Caroline, the new wife, asked the kids to return their keys. She did not want her and her husband's privacy invaded by casual visits from them.

"But," complained Kenneth, "we always know where they're going to be and when, so what difference does it make? We can't be in two places at once!"

"That's not the point, Ken," Caroline countered. "I want to have my things, our things, left the way I want them. I don't like the idea of people rummaging around through our things. They are welcome, of course, to visit when we are in residence, but not when we're not there!"

This was a major battle that led Kenneth to threaten a divorce action. Kenneth was operating from a position of guilt about having left his first marriage in the first place.

An important point in this case study is that Caroline was not in any way involved with Kenneth romantically while he was married to his first wife. As a matter of fact, she had left his employ and spent two years working for a firm in Europe, so she was clear of involvement in the breakup of Kenneth's first marriage. Kenneth simply had not worked through all the emotions of his divorce. Giving his kids keys to his various properties was a way that he felt he could "make it up to them."

In the end, it was Kenneth who asked for the keys, and it was the right move. Now the foursome has a much healthier respect for each other, largely due to Caroline's having stood her ground, and Kenneth was able to free himself from his imagined obligation to form a new "little family."

6. Don't force yourself as a couple on the children This is an easy tool to use. Let yourselves be seen by the kids, no matter whose they may be, as two people who are so secure in their relationship that they don't always have to go around as if they were joined at the hip. It's disconcerting for children, young or old, to see their mom or dad with a person other than their other parent. Watching a lot of emotional and passionate embracing, constant kissing, touching and sitting close beside one another as if there were no other place to sit in the entire room alienates those children. It only makes the going a little rougher for the two of you, and is unnecessary.

After all, everyone knows the two of you have a thing for each other or you wouldn't be together. Use this tool to keep your sensitivity sharpened and to have consideration for the kids. This doesn't mean the two of you have to act like strangers. It simply means you are sensitive to their feelings as they deal with the end of their fantasy about their perfect family.

7. Encourage your partner to spend time alone with his/her children This tool is so valuable because it does two very basic things. One, it enriches and nourishes the relationship the parent partner has with his or her children. Two, it enriches the relationship between the two of you. How, you may ask, does the second benefit occur? When the parent partner is able and willing to spend some time, time without you being present, your mate can get rid of all the pressure he or she may feel about being a "good parent."

63

Elizabeth has never had children, and does not plan to have them. She said, laughing, "God forgot to give me any maternal instinct." Her second husband, Matt, has three grown children near her age.

"As a child of a broken marriage myself," Elizabeth told us, "I know it's important for Matt to spend time with his daughters. I've had several relationships besides my two marriages, but I've also lived alone for long periods of time. I'm comfortable on my own, and I'm comfortable being alone.

"I encourage Matt to spend time with his daughters. Sometimes I even decline invitations that include me so he can be with them on his own. We have them to our house individually and as a group at different times."

Elizabeth continued, "Matt works very hard to continually improve his relationships, and each one is different, with his daughters. I've worked hard to develop my own relationships with them." Again laughing, she said, "Matt is not a piece of furniture. He's got enough love to share with all of us. I get most of his time and attention on a daily basis. I would never begrudge him, or compete for, the time he can spend with his daughters."

Time spent alone with a kid, just being mom or dad, and listening to their problems, hopes, ambitions, and fears sends a message to that child. The parent is saying, "See, I do have time for you, even though I am in an exciting and wonderful relationship!" As for the husband or wife of the parent, he or she will no longer have to watch him or her mope around the house because the parent hasn't spent enough time with the kids.

Use of this tool will almost certainly enhance your age different relationship. You will show that despite your biological age difference, there is a maturity and an under-standing that the joys and obligations of parenthood haven't changed. Once again, it shows security about your relationship.

You can let your partner have the wanted and needed time alone with the children, and know it doesn't threaten your relationship. Rather, it helps strengthen the relationship. You are announcing to all that you have overcome those chains of jealousy that may be interpreted as competition with your partner's children.

These seven tools really work. We strongly encourage you not to forget them or disregard them. Instead, remind yourself of them regularly and you will find yourself using them to your good advantage.

CHAPTER FIVE

Ghost Partners, Part 1: Previous Mates

In the house without you here
Ghosts haunt the halls, the room.
Ghost spouse, ghost cat—
Ghosts of those you loved before
And love a little, a lot, still.
The thought occurs,
"I have this person now
And you, ghost, do not."

You might wonder what impact, if any, previous mates have on an age different relationship. The truth is, they have plenty. Maybe more than plenty, and for reasons that, once they're pointed out, may seem so obvious you could ask, "What made me overlook that before?"

In an age different relationship, the way in which one partner treats their current partner is usually colored by their experiences with someone else from the past. If that someone was near or about the same age, however, then the ways they acted and reacted with each other should be entirely different from such interactions with an age different partner.

The recipe for apple pie we used in the past isn't going to

work when we are trying to make Texas chili today! However, people tend to respond to current situations based on experiences played out on their old tapes from the past, as we have discussed in previous chapters.

If your age different partner is younger, it isn't going to work if you react to various relationship situations as if that partner was just like your previous mate who was the same age. Conversely, if the age different partner is older, then the same applies. Manners and methods that prevailed in a past relationship with a same-age partner just won't work with this new partner. So, often it becomes necessary to explore the roles previous mates had in your "tape library." You must find ways to replace those tapes with new ones that work in your present relationship. To do this, it becomes necessary to talk about previous mates without rancor or jealousy, and this is not easy to do.

To be sure we are playing off the same sheet of music with this idea, let's define what we mean by "previous mates." We would like you to consider this term as applying to anyone from your past with whom you have had a long-term, committed relationship.

We define "relationship" here as a situation between two people in which each remained faithful to their partner and enjoyed sex as well as friendship. Another important qualification is that common goals were set and pursued. You may or may not have married, but a relationship with a previous mate is certainly much more than a few dates or a mere romantic interlude or two.

So, here are some ground rules to be used from the very beginning approaching the topic of previous mates:

1. It is okay to answer questions posed by your current mate. Curiosity is natural.
2. It is *not* okay to compare your past and current mates in any way.

3. Never, but never, ask for comparisons.
4. Teasing may not be okay. Check it out!
5. Forgive absent-minded slips of the tongue; i.e., calling you by the name of the previous mate.
6. Don't engage in or allow ex-mate bashing.

The pitfall around ex-mates is that often they can become "ghost partners" in your present relationship. Let us explain.

Here you are, merrily rolling along in your present relationship, when one of you suggests taking a vacation trip. So far, so good. Then you start to plan where to stay in your chosen resort town. Your present partner suggests a place overlooking the ocean.

" I'd rather not stay there," you reply somewhat meekly.

"Oh?" counters your partner. "And why not, may I ask?"

(Throat clearing) "Well, ah," (more throat clearing), "*she* and I stayed there when we went to San Diego."

"Oh?" comes the offhand, God-how-casual-can-I-be answer. "Well, I guess *she* wins again, huh?"

Thus the ghost partner has made her appearance, and the two of you feel her presence in the room.

Or, consider this scenario: You have settled on a vacation spot and are enjoying same. Your partner seems to sink deeper and deeper into some sort of mood. She seems to be copping an attitude. You confront it, saying, "May I ask what's going on with you?"

"Oh, nothing really."

"Please, I thought our relationship was past that sort of thing. Something's the matter. Now out with it!"

"I guess I was just thinking about when Buddy and I stayed here the time he had a business trip and I joined him for the weekend."

"God, why didn't you say something? We could've stayed someplace else. I don't think I want to stay here myself now, knowing the both of you were here together!"

Fun, huh? Buddy, the ghost partner, shows up on the scene, but this time as the result of a sin of omission. Your partner just conveniently forgot to protest your choice of a place to stay when the two of you made the decision. Instead, Buddy has shown up to ruin things. You must exorcise your ghost partners, not bring them with you into the current relationship.

Kelly and Martin had this exact problem when they decided to marry.

"I'd been married before, twice," Martin told us. "Kelly had traveled quite a bit with men she'd had long-term relationships with, and she had been married before, too."

Kelly laughed. "It seems like it took weeks before we thought of someplace to go on our honeymoon one of us hadn't visited with an ex!"

Martin, also laughing, agreed. "We finally settled on Santa Fe. Now that's one of our favorite places for a vacation. We go back every year on our anniversary. It's our special place together. Neither of us has to deal with memories or worries about ex-mates."

The age different factor becomes apparent when a sore point about an ex-mate comes up and one partner begins to behave parentally again. Such behavior is a sure sign certain issues were not resolved in your mate's previous relationship. You can, however, use several tools to counteract this manuever and keep the relationship on the right track.

1. Make it clear this is *you* talking, asking, declining, or responding, and not the previous partner.
2. Immediately confront the parental mode your partner is demonstrating.
3. Ask, "Is it possible you are playing an old tape here?"
4. Ask, "What did I just say or do that made you reply as if I were _____ (the previous mate)?"
5. Ask, "What do we need to do to make sure it is you and

I who need to solve this, and not you and her/him?"

6. Say, "It sounds like it's scary (or risky or uncomfortable) for you to think of doing this my way. Is it because I am older/younger?"

You can adapt these tools as needed. We give them to you because we know from experience that they work. You can change the language to fit your own style of speaking so the tools feel more comfortable to you. And it is important you realize both of you are going to need to handle situations repeated from earlier relationships so you are ready to use these tools.

Marta, 37, told us she has had a few problems with old tapes from her first marriage with a same-age mate. She has had several relationships with older men since.

"My ex-husband wanted to control everything I did. He wanted to choose my friends, my hobbies, my activities. He criticized my appearance and anything I did or said that he hadn't approved."

Cyn asked, "Is that the reason you prefer older men?"

"Definitely," Marta answered. "I find older men seem more comfortable simply allowing me to be me. The problem I have is automatically reacting to any comments or feedback as if they're trying to tell me what to do."

Marta, then, can adapt one of these tools for use on herself. She can ask herself, for example, "Is it possible *I'm* playing an old tape in this situation?" Sometimes it is difficult initially to be objective enough to use these tools in the heat of a reaction. However, after you've had a chance to cool off, they are excellent aids in learning about yourself and your old tapes. Understanding what causes you to react can empower you to make changes in your reactions.

When there is an age difference, that old material might be so outdated it doesn't even belong in the same room with you. Somehow it still manages to rear its ugly head. It is essential, then, that you not be afraid to confront the *here and now.*

Here and now refers to the time frame within which we want you to deal with each other in your age different relationship. The problem is you or your partner may have a tendency to deal in the *there and then* phase of communications. This is not positive. Think of the *there and then* as being "vertical" communication. This is when the two of you wallow in the past, sinking downward as if you are trying to dig a hole to China through the surface of the earth.

Here and now communications are "horizontal," and flow along the lines of the present. They are panoramic communications, allowing you to move forward, dealing with the present and the future together rather than mucking around in the past. Doesn't that sound much more positive in your relationship, compared to the *there and then* or vertical method?

The issue of previous mates can bring about counterproductive vertical communication in age different relationships. Often, behaviors demonstrated by one partner will remind the other of some earlier behavior. Sometimes this is not the behavior of a previous mate at all, but rather of a child, or worse, a parent in their lives.

A younger woman, Beth, told us, "I always get in trouble with Ben because I don't keep our bedroom spotless. He goes along for awhile and doesn't say anything. Then suddenly he explodes with, 'Jesus Christ, Beth, my eighteen-year-old daughter keeps her bedroom in this same lousy condition!'"

"How does that make you feel?" Cyn asked Beth.

"It makes me feel like I'm the eighteen-year-old daughter, and he's the damn daddy!"

Ben responded with, "I know that Beth isn't a neat freak. I'm not either, but it drives me absolutely crazy when she just has stuff, and I do mean stuff, all over our bedroom. I can't

72

help it, but it reminds me of how Luanne (his daughter) kept her room."

"And I go crazy when you treat me like you're my father!" Beth shot back.

Cyn entered the fray again, asking, "How do you, or how did you, resolve this issue?"

Beth said, "I'm making more of an effort to be neater. But I'm also reminding Ben that I work at a demanding professional job as a teacher, and he needs to pitch in and do more to help me keep our place clean. I just can't, *won't* do it alone."

"She's right there," Ben said. "I haven't done much in our relationship to help with the general housework. We had a maid in my last marriage and I guess I never had to do very much."

"Yeah, well, I'm sure as hell not going to be our maid! Besides, it would be really nice if you would focus on the things I do right to make our relationship work, instead of on what's wrong!"

Beth has a very good point, doesn't she? Concentrating on what is going *right* in your relationship is almost always more important than focusing on what is going wrong. In fact, this is good advice for any relationship. And especially in an age different relationship, in which there are many different pressures—the more you can concentrate on the positive aspects, the better, and the stronger the relationship grows.

This tool is an extension of *here and now* communication. We call it *good and better* communication. Appropriately enough, we call the opposite *bad and worse* communication.

Concentrating on the *good and better* aspects of the relationship means that you are putting a bridle on the tendency to bring ghost partners into the relationship. The *good and better* approach allows you to deal with who each of who you are now. The *bad and worse* focuses on the previous mate and the previous relationship.

Should you find yourself making unfavorable comparisons between your current relationship and one from the past, it may help for you to ask yourself an important question: If your earlier relationship really was great, wouldn't you still be in it? Strive to remember how easily behaviors expressed within the current relationship can trigger old tapes about previous mates. Simple behaviors, dumb issues, and unimportant concerns can trigger either one of you at any time, and the more aware of this fact you are, the better prepared you will be.

Melissa candidly shared her experience with *bad and worse* communication.

"My ex-husband simply didn't like women much. He thought they were all 'sluts'—his words—based on his relationships with his mother and his ex-wife. I didn't understand what was going on at the time, but I've come to understand it better in the years since we divorced."

Jack asked how that made her feel.

"Well, I think when you're treated in a certain way for years, you come to believe you are that way." Melissa thought for a moment, then continued. "I didn't behave like a slut when we were married. But I had dated a lot, slept around some—that was before AIDS. I guess I just started to wonder if I didn't fit the picture my ex-husband had of women in general."

Again, she paused. "I think I began to feel I was maybe inherently 'bad.' That I had to constantly be on guard against my inherent sluttiness."

"How has that affected your current relationship?" we asked. Melissa is engaged to a younger man, John, who is ten years her junior.

"John thinks 'it's okay,' as he says, that I've had other sexual experiences," she answered. "So he jokes about 'all the

74

men' I've had. It's taken me a long time to understand he's not being critical, that he's not indirectly calling me a slut. The fact I'm older and experienced is a turn-on for him. But my first reaction for a long time was to defend myself and my reputation."

"How have you dealt with this issue?" Cyn asked.

"I don't know that I've really dealt with it," Melissa answered. "Over time, as I saw John's confusion about my reaction, I just stopped reacting. I mean, I kept trying to really hear what John was telling me, even though it wasn't what I expected.

"John has a way of encouraging me, supporting me, yet challenging me. I feel like a good person now, largely due to him. I think he's consistently reinforced his opinion of me, even when I didn't feel that way. It's taken both of us to help change something that was essentially my problem. I consider that a sign of his commitment to me, that he would have that patience."

Melissa and John have worked to keep their relationship in the *here and now*, continuing to focus on the *good and better*. Has it worked?

"Definitely," Melissa said. "This is the most rewarding and fulfilling relationship I've ever had, in all ways. I think, I hope, John would say the same."

Following is a checklist of triggers, comparatively small matters that can set off vertical, *bad and worse* communication. How many of them apply to your relationship? How many of them have started your old tapes running about previous mates and ghost partners?

1. He/she *never* picks up clothes.
2. He/she forgets to cap the toothpaste.
3. He/she lets the car get low on gas.
4. He/she is *never* on time.

5. He/she is *always* tired or sick.
6. He/she won't clean the bathroom or sink.
7. He/she *never* empties (or loads) the dishwasher.
8. She leaves her makeup wherever it lays.
9. He/she expects me to do all the cooking.

You can alter trigger number nine by substituting whatever little chore is your particular tape starter. Perhaps your partner is compulsively tidy. Perhaps your partner wants the sheets ironed when it's okay with you if they are simply folded.

Notice that four triggers (one, four, five, and seven) involve the use of *universal* or global words. When you use such words as *always* and *never*, you are speaking as if your partner isn't capable of any change. The implication is that the way he or she acts is totally predictable.

Staying away from universal or global words expands the possibilities of your relationship and opens the doors for change. Particularly in an age different relationship, the abilities to change and invoke change are absolute musts.

Carrie and Ed shared their experience with this problem. Ed told us, "It was difficult for us for a while because Carrie's first husband didn't like sex."

Carrie added, "That's right. He thought it was messy. So he'd masturbate instead, so he could clean up with tissues. It also meant he didn't have to worry about anybody else's satisfaction."

Ed continued, "I have a hard time understanding why anyone wouldn't want to make love to Carrie. I know I almost always want to!"

"What happened for me was that it took me a long time to risk initiating sex," Carrie added.

"And if I'd had a hard day, or didn't feel good, or whatever, she'd feel extremely rejected," Ed said.

Carrie explained, "I just *knew* if he rejected me once, we'd never have sex again. When we married, my first husband was 25 and I was 23. After we married, I think we had sex eight times in five years. Needless to say, I didn't feel very attractive or desirable."

We asked them how they solved their problem.

"I had some comprehension of what was happening for Carrie," Ed answered. "I just tried to keep letting her know I found her attractive and sexy, even when I didn't feel like making love."

"And it worked," Carrie continued. "We changed what you guys call an 'old tape.' I realize now the problem in my first marriage wasn't me. And I know that one 'not tonight' doesn't mean 'no' forever. I never, ever, feel Ed is saying he doesn't want me anymore. Only that occasionally he'd rather snuggle and sleep."

Ed had one last comment. "You know, sometimes Carrie doesn't want to make love either. That had always been a blow to my ego. You know, a virile, sexy older man rejected by a gorgeous young woman. So dealing with all these old tapes has helped us both, I think."

There's no getting around it; you must deal with previous mates and the impact they have on your present relationship. Too often an age different relationship turns sour or unfulfilling because experiences with previous mates wield way too much influence on the present relationship.

When you really think about it, this situation can be very sad, because the experiences you had with a same age or near-same age person are totally different from the experiences of your age different relationship. You simply cannot play a game of football using baseball's rules. They are not the same, and each must have its own exclusive set of standards and procedures.

CHAPTER SIX

Ghost Partners, Part 2: Previous Lovers

We are simply
caught
in each other's webs
and unaware
the disentanglement
takes so much
courage
so many words
and days, weeks,
perhaps even years . . .

What, you might wonder, is the difference between this chapter and the last one? There is a world of difference, and we have discovered this difference between previous mates and previous lovers is even more pronounced when the partners in a relationship are age different.

What makes this so? If indeed ghosts of previous mates have been some trouble to you in your present relationship, how could mere previous lovers be any more trouble? The answer is that pride, ego, and self-esteem are involved. All three of these elements play parts in the discussion of previous lovers. The process of divorcing a previous mate can be a process of completion, while the end of a love affair may often not have such a transition. Therefore, the ghosts of previous lovers might linger longer than even those of previous mates.

This is not to say jealousy and envy aren't also parts of the big picture. Of course they are, but we are discussing the pitfalls of previous lovers at a level above jealousy and envy. While those basic emotions can undermine any relationship, the amount of thought put into pursuing an age different relationship most often means that they have been at least partially dealt with.

With this in mind, let's look at how previous lovers can affect your relationship. We have found in talking to older men, for example, that they can feel threatened by their partner's previous lovers. It doesn't matter how often their partner tries to reassure the troubled mate. The thought is the previous lover must have been better because he was younger.

Looking at the idea objectively, it's really absurd. If the previous lover was so wonderful, what would that person's present mate be doing in the relationship? Ah, well, insecurity does reign supreme in most relationships, age difference notwithstanding.

When we talked to Tony, the insecurity factor became very clear. Tony is only six years older than Cindy, but he is convinced most men she has been with in the past have been better sexually.

"She's told me over and over I'm the best," Tony said. "Still, I can't help thinking she had younger guys who certainly did more for her than I do."

"What do you mean, 'did more for her?'" we asked.

"Well, you know, in the sex department. I just can't handle having sex as much as she wants it. I know men are supposed to be ready any time. But I work hard in a physical job at a packing plant, and I'm tired when I get home."

Cindy had been sitting quietly during the interview until this time. However, she now felt compelled to interrupt her husband.

"I've told Tony—God, I don't know how many times—that he *is* the best man I've ever been with. I just don't know what I can do to convince him anymore! He believes that just because I've been fairly sexually active all my life, I've always been involved with real studs!"

We asked Cindy's feeling about Tony's charge that she wants sex more than he does. We wondered if she thought that has any effect on Tony's feelings of insecurity.

"Yeah, I think it does," she said. "But that doesn't mean Tony doesn't satisfy me, because he does. All the other men I've been with were pretty selfish. Tony is kind and considerate. He cares that I get something out of sex. I would rather have sex once a week, or even once a month, with Tony than have it three times a day with other men I've been with."

Cindy's comment fell right into place with what we were learning about age different relationships. Whether the older partner is male or female does not matter; what matters is that the older partner can bring a sense of calm assurance and a caring and committed attitude to the relationship. This is particularly true when it comes to sex.

Cindy again: "A lot of my past sex experiences with men my own age or younger were 'wham, bam, thank you ma'am' encounters. With Tony, we can spend hours making love and it feels absolutely wonderful!"

An older woman, Rita, told us the one thing she has always felt is great about her present relationship has been sex.

"We have had a bunch of other problems. Money, mostly. But sex has always been great!" Rita said.

We asked her eight-year-younger husband, Will, if he

81

agreed with that.

"Sex with Rita is like nothing I ever thought could happen to me, it's so great," he said. "She really wants to spend a lot of time with sex and with me. I never had a woman my own age who even knew what the hell was going on most of the time sexually. Rita has experience. That bothers me sometimes, you know, wondering how she learned to do what she does. Then she just makes me forget all about that and concentrate on making love."

We asked them both about previous lovers and whether there had been much discussion about them. Rita told us Will encouraged her to talk about her previous affairs. "They seem to be a turn-on of sorts for Will. Am I right, hon?"

"Yeah, I like to hear about Rita's other lovers, or rather her affairs. It makes me sort of live out some fantasies that I've had, but never experienced, if you know what I mean."

"But I absolutely refuse to listen to any of his exploits!" Rita fairly exploded. "I don't want to know who he was with or what they did together. I'm too jealous to even think about Will being with another woman, much less hear about it!"

The spectre of previous lovers can raise other insecurities as well. Pat and Floyd shared one of theirs. Floyd is older by fifteen years.

"Pat's dated some very successful men—an oil executive, a couple of guys who owned their own companies dealing in software and medical supplies. I have my own company, too, but it's not a big moneymaker. Adequate, but we're not talking big bucks."

Pat added, "Sometimes, especially when he's concerned about money, Floyd will make some comment about how I should have stayed with one of those other guys."

Floyd explained, "It just seems she could have had so much more than I can give her. Travel, clothes, furniture, a new car instead of a used one. Sometimes I just feel inadequate that way."

Cyn asked Pat for her reaction.

"I suppose sometimes I just laugh it off when Floyd makes those comments," Pat answered. "The thing about it is, those guys were insecure, too. Maybe about other things. Success doesn't make for happiness. And it definitely doesn't mean the guy is going to treat you well.

"Floyd treats me better than anyone ever has. I don't need more stuff. I do need someone who truly cares about me, listens to me, and puts up with me," she added with a smile.

With a deadpan expression, Floyd said, "Sainthood is a requirement."

Jack asked Pat, "Do you ever regret your past relationships?"

"Not at all," she immediately responded. "Most of the men I dated were fine people, with an exception or two. But I never had the quality of relationship I have with Floyd."

"And I know that's true," Floyd said. "I really do. It's usually when I'm not feeling too good about myself that I think of what she could have had with one of those younger rising stars."

Janey, involved with Eric, who is ten years younger, said she has seen photographs of his ex-girlfriend.

"I'm no dog," Janey said, "but I'm thirty-six and I have a thirty-six-year-old body. You know, a few wrinkles, things sag that didn't used to. Eric's old girlfriend looked like an ad for a health club. Tall, blonde, gorgeous—no sags, no wrinkles, great biceps."

"That's true," Eric said. "But that was all she thought about—her looks and her workouts and her vegetarian diet and her vitamins. Personally, I think Janey's much more beautiful," Eric added as he reached for her hand. "She's smart, she looks great, and she takes time for me."

So we see different aspects of the previous lover spectrum. A previous mate may not be the sexual threat that a previous lover can be. If the older partner already has received some heat around their age different relationship from family or friends, he or she may be extra sensitive about whether or not they are on trial or in competition with past lovers.

The fear of sexual failure is a well-known problem that befalls both men and women, regardless of their age. When the age difference is factored into the relationship, however, these fears may even be more pronounced. The older partner may feel he or she will soon not be able to perform, and that they may not live up to the expectations of the younger mate.

But the older partner is not the only one who might feel inferior to previous lovers. The younger partner can also suffer the same malady.

When Carol and Ben started their relationship, Ben teased Carol about her sexual experience. Ben, twenty years older, had less experience with different people, but longer-term relationships. However, not long after they got together, Ben began to feel guilty about the way his previous relationship had ended.

Carol told us, "Suddenly, it seemed, Ben started talking about this incredible chemistry he'd had with his old girlfriend. I felt terribly threatened, even though I know he didn't do anything like go back to be with her. But I felt absolutely inadequate in every area: sex, looks, money, everything. And there was no way I could compete with incredible chemistry."

"How did you deal with that?" we asked.

Ben answered, "I woke up finally and realized that relationship ended because it was over. And," he added, "I finally realized the chemistry I have with Carol is far more intense."

Thus, both partners can hamper the life they could be enjoying together by allowing experiences with previous lovers to interfere.

Leigh, fifteen years junior to her husband, told us, "I always worry that I won't get it right; you know, do what it is he wants. Sometimes I think he must get tired of teaching me!"

This is a predominant theme we heard from the younger partners. Most of them felt they were in the "learning stages" in their partner's opinion. "It's hard for him not to start 'teaching' me," was a common complaint. We heard the same complaint from a younger man who said his older wife always wanted to show him how sex should be done.

Mattie had a somewhat different perspective on the issue. Not currently involved with anyone, Mattie shared some experiences from her previous relationships with older men.

"Sure, there were times I felt my older partner was conde-scending. Frankly, though, I've had more problems with that from guys closer to my own age. I like older men because they don't seem to mind my previous experience as much. I like to learn different ways of doing things. And I have a lot to offer that older men seem to appreciate more."

Henry is the older mate of Eleanor, whom we introduced in an earlier chapter. Henry talked a lot about the impact his previous lover had on his current relationship and marriage with Eleanor.

"When we first got together, after my breakup with Gloria, Eleanor decided to redecorate my house. She began buying some simple items, like incense candles, and burned them whenever she was in the house. Eleanor told me quite seri-ously that she was going to rid the place of 'whats-her-name.'"

"Well," Eleanor added, "I really believed the ghost of Gloria was still hanging over our relationship. I thought I could do a little exorcism for Henry. You know, something fun that said we both needed to move on in our relationship and eliminate Gloria from our lives."

We asked what had made Gloria such a big issue with them. Eleanor responded by telling us she seemed to do things that triggered Henry to make comparisons.

"Ellie would put her dirty coffee cup on the kitchen counter, right above the empty dishwasher," Henry said. "I told her that was something that really bothered Gloria when I did it, and then Ellie and I would feel a sudden distance between us because I had brought Gloria into the picture."

"That wasn't all of it," Ellie added. "For a while, I thought I could never compete with the memory of Gloria in her relationship with Henry. I began to ask myself, 'if she was so damn great, how come he broke up with her?' We finally had to sit down and really hash it out. We had to get Gloria completely out of the way before we could move on."

This happens often in a relationship in which guilt from the end of a previous relationship is a factor. The anxiety may come from the fear that the partner has used the "leap-frog" method to end an unhappy relationship—that is, the partner has jumped to the current partner to have a good excuse to end the relationship they were in, or to seal its end.

With age different couples, the dragging along of old baggage from previous relationships becomes even more cumbersome. The older partner can tend to be more sensitive to the guilt trap than the younger one, although that's not a rule.

If either partner has not done proper closure with a previous relationship, he or she can lapse into responding to old tapes in the new relationship. They must eventually face what is happening and explore how the previous lover is a ghost partner in the current relationship.

When we talked with Marlene, now separated from her younger lover, she had recently realized she had exited the relationship in such anger that she had been unable to engage in any proper closure around the four years they had shared together.

"Now I just feel guilty as hell that I didn't take his offer for us to go into counseling," Marlene said. "Although I think the outcome would still have been the same. I don't think we would have stayed together, but at least we might have had an opportunity to share how we really felt. As it was, I just pulled out. Now I cry myself to sleep every night because I feel so guilty."

Marlene doesn't yet know the outcome of the separation. She hears rumors her former lover is seeing someone else. In the meantime, they are becoming more polarized as the days of separation turn into weeks and months.

The two partners in an age different relationship may not be the only ones affected by previous lovers. An episode of the television series *Picket Fences* entitled "Thanksgiving," which aired on November 13, 1992, dealt with this subject as it pertains to family members of the older partner. In that episode, the grandfather, approaching seventy, brought his twenty-six-year-old girlfriend to the family Thanksgiving dinner. His daughter, a physician, had a very difficult time accepting the relationship. His son-in-law, as sheriff of the small town, ran a background check on the girlfriend. He found she had been involved with older men before. She had married the last one, who died and left her everything in his will.

The predominant thought everyone had, except the grandchildren, was that the girlfriend was out to get Granddad's money. The daughter was also concerned because her father had heart problems. When she and her husband caught the girlfriend coming from Granddad's room, sweating profusely after obviously having sex with him, the daughter became livid. Clearly, in her mind, the girlfriend was trying to kill Granddad with sex. (By the way, we will discuss family relationships in more depth in a later chapter. The issue here is that the family had trouble accepting this woman's past history of lovers.)

87

The girlfriend confronted the daughter. She explained that she simply preferred older men. Her profuse sweating turned out to be a result of a disease. She had cystic fibrosis, which meant she would probably die before Granddad did.

This was a poignant show, and it brought out an important point. Sometimes families and friends have more trouble accepting the past lovers of a person in an age different relationship than the partners do.

Callie offered her story. "When I started dating Will, who is over twenty years older, my mother wanted my father to come here and break it up. She didn't know Will, but she knew my background with men. It was not great."

Will, Callie's husband, interjected, "It was tough. But Callie had done a lot of work on her own to deal with what I guess we could call past mistakes. But her family didn't trust that."

"What," we asked, "did you do to deal with that issue?"

"Well," Will answered, "I went to South Carolina with Callie and charmed her family with my natural charisma." Will laughed, then continued. "Seriously, it was important for them to meet me and know I meant to do well by their daughter, granddaughter, and sister. Because I did mean to do my best for her, I think the message came through."

"Damn right," Callie interrupted. "Now they all call to talk to Will. Doesn't matter if I'm around. But I know my history of choosing men led them to think I made another lousy choice."

"But she finally got smart!" Will added. "People just don't expect people they know to make changes."

So we see that previous lovers and a person's history with relationships can have an impact on the age different partners and their families and friendships. Sometimes this impact can be difficult to overcome. The message we hope you will take from this chapter is this: remember it may happen. By being aware of the possibility you, your partner, or people you know may have difficulty dealing with the ghosts of previous lovers, you have the power to keep it from having a detrimental effect on your age different relationship.

CHAPTER SEVEN

Housekeeping: The Great Battleground

*i only want to know
    that my being on the planet
    makes a difference
    that there is one person
        in the world
        who would give anything
    to be with me . . .*

Housekeeping *can* be a great battleground, particularly among age different couples. There is something almost eerie at work in situations where housekeeping is the issue. Something brings out the differences between partners in an age different relationship much more dramatically than those between partners of a similar age.

What is that something? We found it was the almost immediate tendency for the older partner to slip into a parental mode when dealing with a younger mate on the subject of housekeeping. Over and over, no matter whether the man or woman was older, we heard comments that sounded as if we were hearing from a frustrated father or

AGE DIFFERENT RELATIONSHIPS

mother instead of a loving, caring, sharing *partner*.

"My God! He never even picks up his dirty shorts from where he's stepped out of them!" Sheila wailed in desperation. "I do three loads of laundry a week just for the two of us. He expects me to run around and pick up his dirty clothes like his mother did!"

"My mother did not pick up after me," Corey said in response.

"Well, then, it was one of your three sisters," Sheila replied sharply.

As soon as we heard this exchange, we knew we were dealing with another age different couple which had positioned opposing troops onto the great battleground of housework.

There was some truth in Sheila's accusations. Corey had been the only boy in a family of four children, and the youngest child. As one occupying that very special position, Corey did indeed have several females playing caretaker for him. At thirty-one, Corey had never served in the military. So whatever habits, good or bad, which he had learned in his childhood with his birth family, he had brought them into his relationship with his wife, Sheila, age forty.

"Sheila bitched about the same things with her first husband," said Corey, rallying to his own defense.

"Well, at least he picked up his own dirty clothes and put them in the hamper. You won't even try to put dirty laundry in the hamper. God forbid that I should ever ask you to help me wash it!"

"I'd be happy to do the laundry, Sheila. But you won't let me. So I don't ask anymore," Corey said.

"Is this true?" we asked.

Sheila moved in her heavy artillery. "Yes, it's true. After the first two times he did laundry I had a pink cast to all my white blouses because he hadn't separated the colors from the whites. You bet I told him to keep his hands off the laundry after that," she fumed.

We asked if there was an opportunity for Sheila to teach Corey how she wanted their laundry done. But Corey quickly bristled in response to Sheila's parental mode with a reply straight out of a child personality.

"Hey, I'm not stupid," he said. "The box of detergent said it was safe for all colors!"

We were obviously moving onto dangerous ground with Sheila and Corey. Further exploration of the laundry subject seemed fruitless. Fortunately, Sheila quickly recovered her composure.

"Corey does do a lot to help around the house. I don't want to give the impression he doesn't do anything," she said. But one area of housekeeping—doing the laundry—was a sore point which brought out their worst behavior.

This was not an isolated case. When we talked with Marilyn, who is younger than Brad by fifteen years, we got the same story, although on a slightly different battlefield.

"She is messier than one of my daughters," Brad said, trying to speak with a playful laugh. It was obvious, however, that Marilyn didn't consider the subject funny.

"Listen, Brad, you knew housekeeping wasn't very high on my priority list when we were dating. You never said a word about it then." Marilyn looked as angry as her voice sounded. "I swear to God, this is the only thing we fight about. I get sick and tired of him compulsively straightening this pile of papers, or fluffing up that pillow, or picking up a pair of shoes I might have kicked off in the living room."

This was Brad's cue to move in a few missile launchers and let fly.

"*Might* have kicked off your shoes? Marilyn thinks every room in the house is her personal wardrobe closet. You can't go in or out of any room in our house and not find some piece of Marilyn's clothing—belts, earrings, shoes, or even a bra!"

"You don't object when I take *off* the bra, you jerk!" laughed Marilyn, breaking the tension. This gave us the chance to backtrack and pursue what made Brad compare his wife's behavior with that of his adult daughters.

"How do you think Marilyn feels when you start treating her like—or at least comparing her to—your daughters?" Brad turned to Marilyn for the answer.

"I don't know," he said. "How *does* that make you feel, Mare?"

"Like I'm not your wife, but one of your daughters. And the thing that gets me down is that I've married two of these compulsive men in my life. Both Brad and my first husband were in the military, and I always accuse Brad of needing to even iron his socks, for God's sake!"

"Oh c'mon, Mare," laughed Brad. "I'm not that bad, am I?"

"Honestly, yes," said Marilyn. "You used to remark how unhappy you were that all your first wife did was clean house, even on days you both had off from work. When you and I were dating, you told me housework didn't matter. You told me you found my other talents to be more valuable to the relationship."

Marilyn took a quick breath and continued. "I feel betrayed somehow, that now after four years of marriage, you suddenly get nutso about cleaning and picking up.

"We have people over. We even have your kids over. Do they ever not find a place to sit, or a table to put their cups on, or do they ever have to eat off of dirty dishes?"

Brad admitted that this had never been the case.

We were interested in Marilyn's statement that Brad had apparently just started his parental houskeeping complaints. We asked what that was all about, and Marilyn responded.

"I work at a very hard job, just like Brad. Except I work *for* someone, while Brad works for himself. I have to work very long hours sometimes, and frankly, I'm bushed when I get home. Housekeeping is just not what I'm ready to do. I need to rest a little, maybe read for awhile.

"Then Brad hits the door, and after some perfunctory greeting and a peck on the cheek, I can see the storm clouds gathering. When I ask him if anything's wrong, he just says, 'No, nothing.' Then he starts banging kitchen cabinets or rattling pots and pans."

"Well, someone needs to be looking after things. I'm just trying to help," protested Brad, although the tone of his voice showed he felt his own position weakening.

"No," Marilyn said emphatically. "You're not trying to help. You're trying to point out some area of housekeeping where I have failed!"

Marilyn and Brad's experience further cemented our belief that housekeeping is an area where the older partner is often most inclined to be parental. Still, Brad did conceed he had been "hitting below the belt" when he compared his wife with his daughters.

"I guess it just brings up old stuff for me," he said. "In my first marriage, I always had to discipline the girls and see that they cleaned their rooms and helped with the chores. Jan, my first wife, was as sloppy as they were. Frankly, it drove me nuts, and it caused a lot of fights between Jan and me."

Old tapes from the past were definitely playing in this situation, as they did when confronting most of the battle-ground issues we encountered in our interviews. Some of the same tools we have proposed in previous chapters can be of use when housework is the problem. (If they sound familiar, that means you're learning them.) Age different couples would do well to adopt or modify these tools in the following way so they can pull their troops off the battlefield of housekeeping and declare peace!

1. Remember, this is your partner, not your child.
2. Design a list of shared chores for both of you, and trade off from time to time.
3. Don't use housework complaints to vent other feelings. (More on this in a moment.)
4. Look for the other things in the relationship that are strong and are working.
5. Remember what brought you together in the first place, and reinforce that.
6. Get rid of the old tapes of parenthood and childhood. Replace them with new relationship tapes which include its rewards, fulfillment, and mutual goals.
7. Ask yourself honestly: is a clean, tidy house what you were hoping your partner would offer?
8. It can also be helpful to ask yourself: what makes the issue of housekeeping so important to you?

The last question is important for both partners—the one proacting and the one reacting alike. However, the questions we present are not necessarily to be answered immediately. In fact, we recommend you *do not* answer them right away.

This may be hard to do, because we are raised in a society that looks for easy answers. We're taught to look for quick answers from our first days in school. But sometimes the value of a question is apparent only after considering it over time, living with the question rather than trying to immediately answer it. In doing so, answers often occur to us that we may not have considered if we had not given the process some time. With this in mind, let's examine one of the tools specifically.

Tool number three is a reference to a behavior described by psychologists as *passive-aggressive*. People who exhibit this kind of behavior habitually resent and oppose others' demands to maintain or increase a given level of functioning, whether at work or in social situations, and they protest by resisting these demands without confronting the issue. Instead, they go underground with their feelings.

If Brad is demanding increased housekeeping efficiency from Marilyn, she might passively obstruct his demands by failing to do her share of the work. She may procrastinate or become inefficient, though she may actually be more capable than even he suspects. She may thwart Brad and his parental attitude by becoming irritable, sulky, and argumentative when he asks her to increase her housekeeping chores. In these ways, Marilyn demonstrates passive-agressive behavior on the housekeeping battlefield.

Sherry, younger by fifteen years than her husband John, shared a story about her passive-aggressive behavior.

"I've been working on my masters degree in nursing," Sherry told us. "It's been two years now. I work full-time, carry a full-time schedule at school, try to raise my kids and have a relationship with my husband." (Sherry has two young children living with her and John.)

"The kids are involved in band and sports. I'm trying to write my thesis on top of everything else. We all do what we can, but right now that's not much in the housekeeping area.

"What I would do, and still do," she said, laughing, "is when John would pressure me about straightening the house, I'd go to sleep. Literally. I'd say I'd do it, but then I'd just get really, really tired and need a nap. Then, at the critical moment before people came over, I'd dump everything in boxes and stack them in rooms we don't let guests go into."

"I've had to change some of my ideas," John said. "I come from a home that was meticulously kept. Our house is clean, but it's messy. It's been difficult for me to accept that."

We asked what he did to adjust.

"I had to ask myself," John answered, "what's more important? To have an active, contributing family whose members are learning to improve themselves and to make a difference in the world, or to have a perfectly neat house?

"We're all out of balance right now," John said. "We all, including me, have a lot going on in our lives. So for now, I think it's more important that we all focus on what's important to each of us—on our jobs, on Sherry's and the kids' school, on learning and growing. Not being able to keep an organized, perfectly straight home is the price we pay for that."

Sherry picked up the theme. "You know, I have always been organized. But I simply can't be the way I used to be anymore. There just isn't time. I hate having books and papers stacked everywhere, but when it comes down to a choice between getting my job done, or writing a paper, or spending time with my family, and cleaning house—well, cleaning house does not win."

There is a great deal to be said for the effect order has on one's ability to concentrate. Chaos is distracting. But then again, every family has to set priorities. Whether you are two or ten, you may have to negotiate these priorities on keeping house.

One question we consider when setting priorities may sound harsh, but it gets down to the bottom line. When your time comes, do you want people to say you kept a clean house, or that you were out in the world doing something that made a difference? Perhaps your answer is something in between. But no matter what the case, you and your partner and your family have to answer for yourselves.

We'll discuss more about differences in lifestyles between age different partners later in this book. However, the responses to our questions about housekeeping confirmed our hypothesis that the older partner tends to be more oriented toward home and family values, while the younger partner is usually more driven to achieve and perform in his or her career. Again, this is not a rule, but rather something we observed quite often, and something to consider.

CHAPTER EIGHT

Marriage vs. Playing House

I begin to see the beauty, the danger, the promise
Of the words "we" and "our" and "us."
I begin to see my life with you will be about
looking at fear, courage, and choice.

That old bugaboo word, "commitment," knocks down all the taboos and traditions like bowling pins. For an age different couple, commitment means getting mature enough, even *bold* enough, to do the big deed—get married.

"So what's wrong with playing house?" you may ask. "What's wrong with trying out the relationship before making it so *permanent?*"

We've made it a policy not to give our readers "right and wrong" kinds of tools. We are not considering this choice as a moral dilemma in this chapter, but rather as an issue which has specific considerations for age different couples.

In an age different relationship, the couple already has a number of factors that are working against them. We have already explored some of these factors with you. But when an age different couple makes it a point to live together and to "try out" the relationship, they simply fuel the suspicions of the people around them who may have raised their eyebrows at the union of the two in the first place. This confirms to them that the age different partners aren't really convinced that their relationship isn't a mistake.

Kim and Stephan were a couple who had discussed living together before marriage. Kim, older by six years, certainly didn't appear to us to be the older partner. We shared our surprise at this discovery.

"I think most people assume that I'm older," said Stephan. "I think the moustache may have something to do with it, and just look at the difference in our sizes."

True, Stephan was a husky, well built six-foot-five man who took significant space in the restaurant booth where we met for breakfast. Kim measured slightly over five feet. She was perky, pert, and had a hairstyle that definitely made her look years younger. Anyone would have difficulty identifying her as the older partner.

"I told Stephan from the beginning that I would not just play house," Kim stated. "But I think he thought I was kidding. I had tried that route before, and my feeling was if I'm good enough to live with, I'm good enough to marry." Stephan had obviously heard this many times before; he and Kim completed the sentence together.

"What is this reluctance to get married?" we asked. "Do you think it is mostly the reluctance of the younger partner, or do you think men want to put off marriage?"

Kim spoke first. "Well, of course, in our case the reluctance to marriage *still* came from this male animal here, but not because of the fact that I am older. I was the one who wanted to get married."

"Yeah, and she never let me forget it!" said Stephan.

We turned our attention to Stephan's reluctance to approach the altar.

"For me, my love for Kim was never a question. She is the greatest thing that ever happened to me. I am simply nuts about her."

"You're simply nuts, period," Kim laughed. "Sorry, I interrupted. Go ahead."

We noted this casual and easy banter between these two from the minute they sat down with us. It was their way of overcoming their nervousness about the interview.

"Well," Stephan continued. "I was worried mostly about what my folks would say. They were pretty upset about this relationship in the first place. If we just lived together, and it didn't work out, they would have understood. But if a marriage didn't work out, that would have been unforgivable."

Kim picked up the cue. "There has never, but never, been a divorce in Stephan's family. I think he was terrified that he would be the first."

They told us Stephan was sure his parents would forgive a relationship with an older woman as being just a "younger man's experiment" or a "folly," as Kim put it. When Kim and Stephan started discussing marriage, however, Stephan's parents were the ones who first suggested they just live together for a while to see how it worked. But Kim's determination won out, and neither Kim nor Stephan have any regrets about not living together before they got married.

When we spoke with Suzanne and Art, we heard a somewhat different perspective.

"It's true, I admit it, I'm a 'Trekkie,'" Suzanne said. "Sometimes I yearn for the opportunity to roam and explore, to see new and different places with no encumbrances.

"I don't need someone to take care of me. I felt I didn't need someone to just be with. If I was ready to settle down with someone, then I'd get married. Otherwise, I planned to explore the universe. I didn't want to just live with someone.

I don't *need* to live with someone. I'd have a commitment with someone I wanted to be married to, or I'd move on.

"I've been accused of seeing life in black and white," she continued, "with no gray areas. I'm not that way about everything, but I am adamant in my feelings about living together versus marriage. I have things to do, places to go, people to meet. I knew I would be married to someone who could support my independence, or I'd remain single."

We were interested in the fact that Suzanne had indeed decided to get married. Art, her husband, and older by twenty years, gave us some more insight into her choice.

"Suzanne is not like anyone I've ever known before," he told us. "For God's sake, she does plumbing repairs! I'm absolutely sure this is not a woman who needs a relationship. She's with me because she wants to be." Laughing, Art added, "I'd be a fool not to do what I need to do to keep her. Plumbers are expensive. And she can paint the house, too!"

Although this time the female partner was younger, it was still her preference to be married. We found in still another case that the male partner was the one who had tried to put the brakes on talk of marriage. Like Art, he was also the older partner, but his reason was a variation on the one we heard from Kim and Stephan. Tom was also concerned about his family; in this case, his adult children.

"If the kids could first accept the fact their dad was just living with someone, I thought it would be easier," he said.

"But when we started talking marriage, they got really depressed," his wife, Julie, added.

We asked what they thought made the idea of marriage so depressing for the kids.

Julie said, "It's no secret. I get along with the boys really well. The two girls have taken their time forming a relationship with me, but I've always known they have a deep relationship with their mother. They protect her a lot."

We filled in the rest. If Julie and Tom just lived together, the kids could handle that. But marriage would destroy their lingering fantasy forever. What fantasy? The two girls still believed their mom and dad might get back together someday. Their father's marriage with Julie, however, would put the proverbial spike in the vampire's heart. Their remarriage fantasy would die forever.

Tom explained their choice. "I realized I couldn't live the rest of my life based on my children's fantasies. It was not easy, but I knew that it was important that they understand life doesn't always work they way they want it to. I'm happy with Julie, and I think a happy father is a great gift to offer my kids."

Francine and Jeremy didn't marry, nor did they make it as a couple. He is fifty-five and married to another woman. She is engaged to marry, and at forty-one, this will be her second marriage. Francine and Jeremy did not, of course, talk to us as a couple. However, we had learned of their on-again, off-again relationship from still another age different couple. We contacted Francine first, then Jeremy.

Francine told us that she would describe their five year relationship as turbulent, even destructive. "At first, the fact that Jeremy was fourteen years older than me wasn't an issue," she said. "But as the relationship became more strained, I began to see that those fourteen years were putting their own 'black magic' on us."

She went on to explain Jeremy became more stubborn as time went on, which bothered her and made her think he was getting what she described as "crotchety." Cyn confronted Jeremy with this statement in a later interview, and he laughed.

"Any opinion that didn't agree with Francine's she attributed to my being older and intolerant," he told Cyn. We had asked Francine if they had planned to marry.

"I think he was more interested in that than I was," she answered. "I don't mean I wanted to go on just living together, but I was content to wait and not rush into marriage. We were both fresh out of recent divorces."

What we determined had happened between Francine and Jeremy gave us another topic in the "pitfall" category. The clue was in that last statement of Francine's—both partners had recently been divorced.

Any person, regardless of age, needs to have time and be willing to grieve the loss of the previous relationship. Too many people jump into a new relationship without really cleaning up the emotional mess from the last one. If a person does not do closure on a past relationship, he or she will simply repeat the errors of the past with a new person.

Often, an older or younger partner can offer a special kind of validation of one's value, beauty, or intelligence. At the end of a relationship, especially of a fairly long-term and intimate relationship, we may tend to look for exactly what was missing, and find it in an age different relationship. The missing ingredient might be a sense of feeling attractive, exciting, intelligent, or of value. While there is certainly no harm in looking for the validation that might have been missing in the relationship recently ended, the danger is in expecting someone of a different age to permanently provide that missing ingredient before you have an opportunity to see if you can find it for yourself.

What caught our attention with Francine and Jeremy was how their age difference was reflected in their problems of not completely resolving relationships with previous mates.

"Jeremy was, and is, I think, a lot needier than I am. To him, marriage was a way of making sure that he would have a wife when he got even older," Francine suggested. "I was anxious that we eventually make it permanent, but I wasn't in as big a hurry."

We asked her for her reasons.

"I realize now I hadn't really ended with my first husband. We were married for fifteen years, had four kids together, and he left me, moved out of the state, and quickly remarried."

Francine spoke of her first husband's alcoholism as being the reason she had initiated divorce proceedings and ultimately ended their marriage.

"He tried treatment but quit, then moved to Seattle where he was sure he could control his drinking," she said. "Jeremy suddenly showed up at the church I attended soon after that. He acted with so much self-assurance that I was bowled over. I really didn't even know what hit me. I guess I was really vulnerable, and this very handsome older man just swept me off my feet."

Francine told us that life with Jeremy was absolutely ecstatic for her at first. They didn't live together, since two of her children were attending local colleges and still lived with her. She was anxious to preserve what she termed a "sense of dignity."

"My kids knew Jeremy was older. But God, he was handsome, had a great sense of humor, and treated me and my kids like we were precious jewels," she said. "It was very much a sexual, whirlwind affair that blossomed into what I thought was becoming a long-term relationship."

"Oh yes, it was passion, passion, passion," Jeremy laughed during our interview over breakfast. "I had never met anyone, at least that I could recall, who had sparked that drive in me. I was coming out of an eight-year marriage I had rebounded into after my first marriage of eighteen years had ended. I think I was pretty anxious to make up for lost time. Francine was absolutely fireworks in bed," he told us. He also said he had no children of his own, and had taken to hers "big time," as he put it.

"But when I would talk about moving in together, things

107

fell apart," he remembered. "Francine was always talking about the kids' father and how he might cause trouble if she moved too quickly. Since she was divorced and her ex-husband was in another state, I was confused about how this guy could cause trouble," Jeremy said. "What this turned out to be was Francine's fear her kids would be turned against her by her ex's criticism of our relationship, especially since I was older."

We learned that Francine had a very tumultuous relationship with her father, one that had never been resolved. Her ex kept claiming that Jeremy was "just another father" to Francine. Her children picked up this theme, and it became a wedge between her and Jeremy.

"We looked at new houses together, thinking that if we made a commitment—you know, really made a commitment like marriage—then things would smooth out," Jeremy told us.

Things didn't smooth out. Francine moved in with Jeremy, but then, guilt-ridden by the failure of her first marriage and her stormy relationship with her father, she moved out.

"We'd go for several days without speaking to or seeing each other," Jeremy explained. The relationship would be over. Then she or I would break down. I would find a flower on my car dashboard. Or I would buy a cute plush animal and send it to her office. Soon we'd be together again, and Francine would move back in."

Francine's children were old enough that they pretty much lived their own lives. They visited what was now essentially a vacation home where they could come and go as they pleased, since their mother was living with Jeremy yet had no plans to sell her house.

Francine told us, "We would have periods when we were absolutely crazy in love. Then Jeremy would show me his old, rotten habits, and I began to believe in that saying,

108

'You can't teach an old dog new tricks.'"

Jeremy and Francine obviously assessed the problems in their relationship differently. Francine spoke of Jeremy's sloppy housekeeping and personal hygiene habits which, she said, "absolutely drove me nuts." Jeremy, however, denounced Francine's "obsession" with how neat her first husband was. "I always thought I was a pretty neat guy, but Francine produced a list of over one hundred bad habits she had seen in me. It pissed me off so much that we fought, and she packed and moved back to her own house again," Jeremy said.

We sensed we might not ever get the real story—it was impossible to interview the two of them together. It was, however, clear that Francine may have been using Jeremy's age as an excuse for their breakup, telling herself she did not want someone who reminded her of her father. She may also have wanted someone very different from a very neat, orderly and dominant personality like her ex-husband at first, only to end up trying to remake her new love into a clone of him.

Francine had one last rather bitter remark at the conclusion of the interview. It was a statement which would justify in her mind forever that Jeremy's age was the real reason they hadn't married.

"I hadn't been gone from Jeremy's house even a month even before he was living with a young teacher he had met. They were married less than six months after that. I guess he finally found his retirement plan in her. They're still married." This statement reinforced Francine's original belief that Jeremy had seen her as partner who would support him in his old age.

While the story of Francine and Jeremy is unique in many ways, it exemplifies a common observation: playing house can be a convenient way to enter a relationship and be free to exit it when problems arise. Instead of identifying the specific problems and finding and implementing solutions—procedures the commitment of marriage might promote—this couple simply found it easier to break up. They left their specific problems right where they lay, on the floor of a broken relationship.

Here are some questions couples can ask themselves when thinking about marriage versus playing house:

1. *What's keeping us from committing to a more perma-nent living arrangement?*
2. *What problems are we having that living together can resolve or is resolving?*
3. *Would the commitment of marriage help us solve these problems in a more effective manner?*
4. *Is our age difference making our decision for us? If so, how?*
5. *Would we play house if we were a same age couple? If so, what would the reasons be?*
6. *Does marriage scare us because we are age different?*
7. *Are we preoccupied with who will need to care for whom if we marry?*

On the lighter side of this issue, a recently married friend shared an anecdote with us.

"I must have been about six years old," Connie told us, "when I fell in love with a younger man next door. He was about four," she chuckled. "We got 'married' about every other day. Sadly, though, we never played house, or doctor either, for that matter.

"I didn't always go with younger men. But now that I'm in my prime," Connie laughed, "I find men my own age tend to be boring. I love to dance, to go out now and then, and be active. Most men my own age seem to have given up on fun.

"Ted wanted to be here, but couldn't because of business. I think he'd agree, though, that we have a great marriage. We do have fun. Just because I'm forty-five and he's thirty-seven doesn't mean we have nothing in common. Au contraire—we have almost everything in common."

We asked if Connie and Ted had lived together before their marriage.

"No, actually, we didn't. And that was his choice, really. I would have, I think. But Ted wanted something permanent. He didn't have any problem with commitment," she said. "But I was worried about what would happen years from now, when I might be old and infirm and he wouldn't. I didn't want someone with active years of life left to live have to take care of me."

We asked what changed her mind.

"Ted," Connie answered promptly. "He asked what made me think the same scenario wouldn't happen if we were the same age. He also pointed out that he could become ill and I might have to take care of him. And then he said, 'who knows what's going to happen—let's have a good time for one day at a time.' That's when he asked me to marry him." Connie laughed, and said, "I thought about it, oh, maybe five seconds."

She finished by saying, "See, he's right. None of us knows what's going to happen. That's why I married him." She smiled. "He's smart, and man, can he dance!"

Certainly we would not presume to insist that every couple must be married to have a satisfying relationship. All we pose is this question: Is marriage *not* being considered because of a fear of commitment? Further, would your relationship be strengthened by marriage? If so, isn't that really the bottom line?

CHAPTER NINE

In-Laws and Other Relations

I remember Saturday nights
you would read to me . . .
Can you know how much
your gifts are part of my life?
Can you hear my thank you
for teaching me how to love?

After you make a stab at dealing with your and/or your partner's kids, you're ready for a whole different set of problems. If you're the older partner, what will it be like to have a mother-in-law or father-in-law that is nearer your own age? How will it be for them to introduce you as their son's or daughter's mate? And no matter if you are the older or younger partner, how will your new sisters-in-law or brothers-in-law feel and act?

A woman—we'll call her Bev—may not think twice about introducing her sister's older husband as "my brother-in-law." However, Bev's parents may be uncomfortable introducing someone their own age as their son-in-law. And Bev's sister never introduces herself as stepmother to her husband's children, who are within five to seven years of her age. We find it to be a pretty consistent practice for older adult children to refer to their mother's or father's mate as "my mother's husband" or "my father's wife."

This, of course, frequently applies even when there is no age difference. It is appropriate behavior for everyone involved, particularly when we keep in mind the consequences of trying to put together another "little family."

When an age different couple takes their place in the family circles of each partner, family members can display some rather obvious yet strange behaviors:

1. There can be a tendency for parents of both partners to side with the older mate, even when it seems obvious that the younger mate may be defending a more sensible and forthright position. This seems to be an "age-bonding kind of thing," according to one of the couples we interviewed.

2. Parenting behaviors tend to be passed on from both sets of parents to the older mate. Again, this was attributed to the same "age-bonding."

3. Grandparents are generally much more tolerant of, and in support of, age different relationships than parents. One woman said she believed this was because her grandparents were more concerned about her happiness than about appearances, and more accepting of the age of her older mate.

4. Siblings of either mate can be very judgmental at the beginning of the age different relationship. Later, however, they often become strong advocates of the relationship, particularly as they see their sibling's continued happiness.

To help along the adjustment with their new extended families, couples who are age different may need to say to the families, directly or indirectly, some or all of the following:

114

"Please accept us for what we are to one another, not for what you may think we are."

"Understand that we are constantly growing in our relationship because we must. We ask you to grow with us by being open to the idea of change."

"You may wonder how our relationship is different, how it is better. Please don't pry into it. We have made significant, sometimes difficult, choices in order to be together, and ask for your support."

"Jokes or good-natured kidding about us are fine if we are involved. Being the brunt of such behavior and comments, however, is not acceptable to us. We'd rather you let us set the tone of any humor."

Some of these statements have been used by couples we interviewed, and their experiences confirm that they lead to increased support from family members, especially after marriage. However, the concerns that are not being openly stated—the so-called passive-aggressive behaviors of family members—are another matter. They are the potential saboteurs of an age different relationship, and usually need special attention.

For example, say the female partner's mom and dad agree to come to dinner. Mom, however, is uncomfortable with her daughter's relationship with an older man, although she refuses to say so. Two hours before dinner, mom develops a terrible headache. This, of course, causes the parents to cancel the dinner date for that night. Mom's passive-aggressive behavior won't allow her to even talk with her daughter about how she really feels. Instead, the headache protects her from dealing with an uncomfortable situation.

Should such behaviors continue to occur, and should they go unchallenged, there is definitely a storm brewing in the family. It is best to sit down and discuss the problem. Try to communicate on a feeling level during the conversation.

The age different couple needs to confront the reluctant parent(s), but in a constructive way. Try using these tools:

1. Say, "Mom and/or Dad, I feel you don't like or approve of my relationship. Can you tell me what's making me feel this way?"
2. Ask, "Mom and/or Dad, what could we do to help you feel differently about us? First, though, let us point out that ending the relationship is not a viable option for anyone else to choose for us."
3. Don't let them get by with a statement like "I just feel uncomfortable." A good way of getting around this is to ask: "If either of you are feeling uncomfortable, can you tell us exactly what that means?
4. If no dinner plans have been made, you might make the following suggestion: "Could we all sit down together and talk openly about this?"
5. If you sense some hidden feelings in family members, you might ask: "Is our age difference the only reason you seem hesitant to accept us as a couple? Is there something else we could look at?"

"Looking at" is a polite way of saying that you and your mate are willing to examine openly any aspect of the relationship that is bothering your relative. You are also saying you have faith and confidence in the relationship, and that you are unafraid to expose it to further scrutiny. This offers a setting within which you and your mate can familiarize family members with your relationship. You can discuss how you got together in the first place, the dynamics between you, and especially the strengths each of you brings to the relationship.

The questionnaires we used as an initial contact to couples we would interview asked about the reaction of relatives to the relationship. We were impressed that the majority stressed that they received unqualified support from their families. Those who responded negatively often did not have living parents, or were estranged from their relatives. In personal interviews, these couples would often add, "I know my mother and father would love him (or her) as much as I do." The fact that few of the couples we spoke to had difficulties with extended family members may be a sign that age different relationships are becoming more widely accepted. Of course, this does little to console the couple whose families are proving to be resistant.

An interesting family dynamic occurs when you have what we call an age different case of "mistaken identity." We saw an example of this dynamic with Lois and Bob.

Bob is the older mate in the relationship by ten years. Lois has two slightly younger siblings, and both her parents are living. Lois also has a remarkably spry eighty-one-year-old grandmother. Bob, an only child, has no living parents and no relatives other than first cousins. He has not seen nor spoken with them in several years.

Both Lois and Bob told us of how well they got along with her family and how well their marriage was received by her family. Lois's father and mother had both attended their wedding. Lois had been married before, but she had eloped. So it was with great pride that Lois's father gave away the bride when she married Bob. Everything was wonderful, according to Bob, until Lois's sister Lynda began to seek Bob's advice about investments.

The "mistaken identity" dynamic was set into motion as Lois's father began to feel left out. He was somewhat angry because his daughter was turning away from him and his advice and seeking advice from her brother-in-law instead. Bob felt very uncomfortable with this situation, and told Lynda so.

"She made light of my concerns," Bob said. "She said her

AGE DIFFERENT RELATIONSHIPS

dad had always encouraged her to get second opinions on everything, particularly investments, so he should have no problem."

"Bob was right about Dad's hurt feelings," said Lois, "though Dad had started Lynda out with a small investment grubstake, as he had done for me and Robbie, our brother. When Bob came into my life—our lives—Lynda started getting advice from Bob, and it hurt Dad a lot."

Bob solved the problem by ending the "mistaken identity" pitfall that Lynda had provoked. She was blurring the roles of Bob and her father, at least in her dad's eyes. While she thought what she was doing was harmless, and actually was not conscious of the consequences, others realized it would cause a breach in several family relationships; Lynda and her father would be at odds. Soon Bob and her father would begin walking on eggshells around each other. Then Bob and Lois would begin to have difficulty over the issue if they were forced into the position of having to choose sides. And if the investment advice Bob offered turned sour for Lynda, she and Bob might have a falling out.

Bob suggested that he and Lynda together ask her father for his opinion on her investments.

Bob said, "I told Lynda what I thought would be good for her money when it came time to roll her C.D.s. I also said it would be a really great idea to ask her Dad what his suggestions were, and that we should do that together."

Bob carried out his plan. Lynda and Lois saw their dad shine at having everyone seek his opinion. He ended up supporting Bob's suggestions for Lynda's investment, and everyone won.

Had the "mistaken identity" been allowed to continue, there would have been lots of losers.

Ann and Brent had a similar problem. Ann and her mother had always been very close. When Ann married

Brent, however, who was an older man, she turned to her spouse for emotional support.

"Mother was really unwilling or unable to discuss the distance that suddenly seemed to develop between us," Ann said. "I would call to talk, and Mother wouldn't really show much interest in what I had to say. That was a real change from before my marriage."

Bob added, "I'm a psychologist, so it was natural for Ann to ask my input on any problems she might have at work. Before, she always used her mother as a sounding board, or a shoulder to cry on. And her mother was always there."

It took Ann a while to understand what was happening. Her mother no longer felt needed, and rather than help her relationship with Ann to change and evolve, she withdrew. Once Ann saw what was happening, she no longer felt the rejection she had felt initially. She made an extra effort to share more about her life with her mother. The process took time and persistence on Ann's part before her mother began to feel she was important in her daughter's life again.

Resolving issues with family members (or for that matter, with anyone important to either of you) may take time if they are having difficulty accepting your age different relationship. The keys are patience and a strong sense of commitment to your mate, and an understanding that you want *all* your relationships to work.

CHAPTER TEN

Careers: Yours and Mine

Stark white paper scattered
like trash by the wind
errant pens and pencils
creeping from their boxes
black ringed binders
capturing wayward reports
holding them hostage
for payday ransom

Any partners in a relationship, regardless of their ages, may have difficulties around the pursuit of their individual careers. After all, being involved in a committed relationship does not mean that either partner stops having a career or trying to achieve personal goals.

However, when there is an age difference, some entirely different kinds of pressures enter the scene, and they can be troublesome. In this chapter we will identify some of those "hot spots," and show you strategies to avoid or overcome them.

121

Often the most troublesome career-related area for the couple is time; more specifically, the time spent away from the relationship while the younger partner pursues his or her career goals. If the older partner was able to take the time necessary for achievement in a career, it seems fair the younger partner should have the same opportunity.

The obvious problem is, of course, that the older partner was not in the present relationship during those career-building years. Now he or she is ready to enjoy the wonders of the current relationship, possibly without expecting to make sacrifices for his or her mate's career plans.

"Whaddaya mean you're going to be in class two nights a week and Saturday mornings?" is not an uncommon cry in some age different households. Perhaps the younger partner, sick of a dead-end job, has decided to start or complete a college degree. He or she selects one of the outstanding programs that allow adults to work on degree programs at night and on weekends while continuing their existing jobs and lives.

But suddenly, this decision affects the relationship. Maybe he or she had a standing Saturday morning breakfast date with the other person, weekly tennis or racquetball dates, regular workout sessions, or some other routine. Whatever it was may now have to be drastically altered to accomodate the new school and/or career plan of the younger partner.

We'll be discussing how to deal with this situation in a moment, but before we do, we want to be sure we don't give you the impression it's always the younger partner who may want to advance or change careers. Let us add that a new phenomenon has entered the American work scene: early retirement.

Now more than ever, companies are looking at ways to reduce the high costs of vested pension plans, benefits to long-term employees, and perhaps most of all, the higher salaries that a company's long-term employees command.

This means an increased possibility that the older partner might be the one who must look at a career change; he or she might have to do something different to be employable somewhere else after being unceremoniously handed a "golden parachute" and told to jump from the corporate plane.

"I sure wasn't ready for retirement," Ted told us. "At fifty-four, even if I had the money to do so, I think I would have gone absolutely nuts without a full-time job."

His younger spouse, Billie, spoke up. "I married him for better or for worse, but not for lunch! My mother said that to my dad when he was wanting to take early retirement. Dad decided to ride it out because he realized that he would probably just be a burden around the house."

Retirement can be something rewarding. It should not mean simply "sitting around the house." Retirement can be a reward for a lifetime of hard work, but some preparation for it is necessary. One must be ready, and in an age different relationship, remember your partner must be ready as well.

Here we have another "hot spot" that can creep into an age different relationship. Billie was pretty much equating her husband's situation with her father's early retirement wishes. She was seeing Ted as her father, and was adding pressure to Ted's desire to not "just sit around." Her emphasis was that she wasn't going to tolerate that.

Billie was making a common mistake in her thinking. We must treat ourselves as who we are now: a new couple with our own particular set of problems, and with new possibilities that may not have been legitimate alternatives before. Ted had no desire to retire; he wanted to consider studying for the law school entrance exams and try to enter law school.

"So what do I have to lose?" he asked us. "I'll be spending

the next few years doing something. It might as well be doing something I always wanted do, like going to law school."

"Do you want to practice law when you graduate?" we asked.

"I don't know. I realize that some firms, maybe most firms, will be reluctant to hire a lawyer with no experience who will be pressing sixty before ever being in a courtroom. However, a law degree combined with my thirty years of executive experience in telecommunications makes an interesting package for a lot of corporations. At least that's what I'm banking on."

Billie added, "I think Ted would make a great lawyer. I also think it's possible he might enter politics, especially since he doesn't even begin to look his real age. A law degree seems to be a real plus for a politician."

Ted hasn't made a final decision whether or not to pursue this new dream, but this story illustrates that an older partner may also need to devote time to the pursuit of a new career.

Now let's return to a situation where the younger partner wants to pursue a new career path. Shirley and Ken are a good example. Shirley, the younger partner, decided she needed to get an advanced degree to help her move out of the employment valley in which she felt trapped.

"It was certainly an adjustment for our family when Shirley decided to get her MBA," said Ken.

"What was the biggest change?" we asked.

Ken pondered his answer for a moment. "Well, there were actually two problems. One, I had been using Shirl a whole lot in my accounting firm. She has her own clients and has generated a lot of business for the firm. She had to turn over those clients to someone else because of her school load."

"Well, that's not entirely true, Ken," Shirley responded. "The clients I brought into the firm on my own, I have kept pretty well in my basket. Tax time will be a problem, but I can make it work. The clients I 'handed off,' as you put it, had not yet built any kind of personal relationship with me. Anyone in the office could handle their files."

Ken neither denied nor confirmed what Shirley said. Instead, he continued with, "The second problem was what was happening at home. Shirl had always been home before I arrived, so most nights she could exercise our dog and start on dinner. All that changed with her school schedule, because she just isn't there to do stuff."

"Well, Ken, this talk about 'doing stuff' sounds like what is really important in our relationship is my ability to walk the dog and prepare the meals. I have a real problem with that!"

He replied, "That isn't what I intended to say, Shirl. I simply meant these were additional chores that were now up to me. It was something I hadn't really been prepared for."

Ken and Shirley were adapting to their new situation, and both recognized it would take time and understanding. Many couples we talked to could relate to this. Here's one composite scenario, drawn from several different experiences of age different couples:

When Megan decided she wanted to finish her undergraduate degree, she and husband Josh talked about what it would mean to the relationship. Meg had always given top priority to the quality of the relationship, something Josh also defined as number one on his list.

Megan began to explore the possibilites of colleges and universities in their area. She chose a program at an outstanding local college to complete her undergraduate degree in Computer Sciences. This meant that she would be in class at least two nights a week and some Saturday mornings. This was going to be disruptive to a routine she and Josh had established.

Josh, an architecht, rarely finished seeing clients until after eight o'clock p.m. Then he and Megan would eat together, "fashionably late." Megan's school commitment now meant he would eat alone at least twice a week. It also meant the two of them would have to give up their Saturday morning breakfasts out, a practice they had steadfastly maintained as a way of catching up with each other on the week's events.

They discussed trying to have breakfast before Meg had to be on campus, and sometimes that worked. More often than not, however, it was just too difficult to manage.

"Josh began to show some resentment of my schedule," said Megan. "Still, I knew he was trying to be supportive of my new career path goals." To put the situation in perspective, let's list what Megan was now trying to do:

1. Maintain and support a quality relationship;
2. Maintain a full-time, demanding job; and
3. Take a full schedule of classes at night and on Saturday mornings.

What Megan and Josh needed was a set of tools and warning signs which we found serve as reference points for the ways we had reacted and needed to react when Cyn started work on her two degrees. These tools and warning signs are:

1. The Guilt Trip Warning Sign
2. Recharging Time
3. The Double Messages Warning Sign
5. Sharing Goals
6. Sharing Rewards
4. Reprioritizing, and
7. Planning Special Nights

126

Now, here's how they apply:

The Guilt Trip is often the first warning signal that comes into play. Josh *was* supportive of Megan's efforts, and often told her so. When Meg would remind him of the hours of study or homework a particular class required, Josh would assure her she should "take all the time she needed."

Josh would then make plans with other people to do things that he and Megan had enjoyed doing together, or simply indicate there was an event or some project he wanted both of them to do. In these ways, he was sabotoging the time frames Meg had set aside to study. Megan, feeling guilty, would give in, and join Josh in the activities, only to work all night to make up for the study time she had missed.

At first the couple was unaware that this was the Guilt Trip at work. When it dawned on them, they took steps to correct it. Josh began waiting to make plans which would include Meg until she gave him some clue that she was ready for some "Recharging Time."

Recharging Time is a simple concept. For Megan, it might have meant putting away all the school books and treating herself to a day as a "couch potato," reading fiction, magazines, or just sleeping. Sometimes it meant being social and spending time with Josh and their friends. Whatever form it took, Recharge Time was an important tool for them to use. It gave Josh a better appreciation of the demands on Meg, and it helped eliminate many of the problems the Guilt Trip warning sign had provoked.

Another of the warning signs Megan and Josh experienced was the *Double Message*. Josh was *telling* Meg he was really supportive of what she was doing. However, his flashes of resentment were shown by a second message saying, "I really don't want you to spend this much time on something for yourself."

127

Watch for this warning, and confront the underlying message as soon as it appears. An age different couple cannot afford to let such issues go unresolved, because this leads to the danger of either partner playing old tapes and stuffing their anger, thus causing damage to a relationship that is otherwise succeeding. What we might describe as "conventional" relationships may be able to afford the luxury of an unresolved issue; this is often not the case with an age different relationship.

When we look at the *Sharing Goals* tool, we see that help is available in avoiding guilt trips and double messages. Cyn has often joked with Jack about "being his retirement plan." In a lighthearted way, this allows both of us to share her goals of using her advanced degree to improve our lives when Jack may not want to maintain the rigorous work schedule he now pursues. This is a form of sharing goals.

Josh needed to be more involved in the ultimate goals Megan was setting for herself. When he did so, he became more supportive and stopped delivering double messages.

Once a couple learns to share goals, they need to be ready to *Share Rewards*.

School functions where a husband and wife can get to know a spouse's new friends can be great ways to enjoy this tool. The obvious pride of graduations, awards ceremonies, and all functions that recognize the work of the partner can and should be shared.

When the age different couple runs into a schedule bind caused by career upgrading, it is time for them to *Reprioritize*. This means that couples such as Josh and Megan had to recognize they couldn't keep operating under the old priorities of their relationship. They had to establish new priorities, emphasizing the time required for Megan to attend school, study, and to recharge. As they did so, they kept in mind that the future rewards would benefit them as a couple.

Reprioritizing also means looking seriously at your social life together. Josh and Meg had been season ticket subscribers to a local theatre for several years. In fact, this was one of the activities that had brought them together in the first place.

"We simply faced the fact we should not renew our seats for another year," Josh said. "We were scheduled for just too many theatre dates. On Fridays, Meg would work a full day at her job, dash home and change, and we'd grab dinner and hurry to the theatre."

"So far, that's no different from what many couples do," Megan commented. "But the real kicker was I had to be in a four-hour class early the next day, and I mean seven-thirty in the morning early! It was simply too much, and we weren't enjoying the theatre or each other."

"Something had to go. We decided to drop out of the theatre season until Meg finished school," said Josh.

What they had done was reprioritize for the sake of the relationship. In view of all the pressures on Meg that came with improving her career opportunities, it was obvious the old game plan they had as a couple would no longer work.

Thus, *Special Nights* become important for an age different couple as a means of keeping their perspective on their relationship. They also help the person who is focusing more on their career not to feel so guilty. The guilt can come from the awareness of the time taken away from the relationship, time the more career-secure partner may resent. This resentment often stems from the fact that he or she already has a career and may not fully appreciate the time demands and pressure on the other partner.

We found that most couples in this situation (including ourselves) have experienced this friction regarding the demands on a partner's time. Too many years may have passed since the older partner last sat in a classroom, prepared a term paper, studied for finals, or attended small group study sessions. As a result, resentment has a way of creeping into the relationship even when both partners have the best intentions. This resentment can force a choice between a new or improved career and the relationship, and that is not a choice which should have to be made.

So, during Special Nights, all books, papers, study groups, and even talk of school or career pursuits is put aside. The couple concentrates on each other. They should return to the basics of their relationship and share those activities that brought them together in the first place. Here's what we've done on Special Nights, whether we were able to plan them weekly or every other week. (We began trying to make Saturday our Special Night, but we often opted to shift to Sunday if that fit our busy schedules better.)

These Special Nights included such activities as:

1. Planning and cooking a meal together.
2. Going out to dinner.
3. Going to a movie, often at matinee times to save money.
4. Enjoying a romantic evening at home, which included no phone calls and no interruptions. Candlelight, music, and sharing a bubblebath were some of the things we included in our evening.
5. Having a movie festival, during which we rented several videos, made a huge bowl of popcorn, and generally indulged ourselves.
6. Mall crawling, just for the fun of it, not necessarily to buy anything.

You can certainly create your own special activities. The important thing is to make your Special Nights a priority, no matter what shared activities you choose. They are a way to recharge and nourish the relationship, to reaffirm the goals you both share, and to bolster the career advancement choices of either partner.

So far we've talked almost exclusively about the problems inherent in continuing education, a phenomenon which is becoming more common as businesses and the economy change. However, the coping principles we've discussed also apply to any dual-career marriage between age different partners. As we've pointed out, often the older partner has established his or her career while the younger partner is still climbing the career ladder.

"Becky has a well-established career and clientele," Peter told us. "She's worked hard for many years, and she's very successful. I, however, still need to do a lot of work to establish my practice and to develop it to the level I want."

Peter is a certified public accountant, and Becky is a real estate agent. Becky has been successful despite the economic recession during the past few years, while Peter has struggled to maintain and develop his practice. Peter is fifteen years younger than Becky.

"Peter works incredibly long hours," Becky said. "I often resent the time he puts into his practice, especially during tax time." She seemed to consider her thoughts for a moment, then continued. "I can think back to a similar point in my career, and I know that I worked long hours and put a great deal of effort into my job, so I can't blame Peter for doing the same thing at this time in his career. I was a single mother with two children, and I felt it was absolutely necessary that I be successful. I think Peter feels the same way, but maybe for different reasons."

"That's true," Peter said. "I need to know I can be successful on my own. Becky knows the feeling—we've discussed it. Still, now and then we have these conflicts that stem from the time I spend on work, time she no longer has to spend on hers."

Peter and Becky know that the resentments will probably resurface every so often, but they are confident with the knowledge they can deal with them as they come up.

The tools we've discussed are useful in dealing with almost all career conflicts. We have used them effectively in continuing education and career advancement circumstances for both of us. However, this is not to say it's easy. It is *not* easy, and this is where commitment to the relationship becomes extremely important. Confronting issues such as feeling neglected and dealing with the fact that some degree of neglect may be temporarily necessary to the long-term achievement of one's goals are difficult. The decision about the degree to which time spent on your relationship will take precedence, and the negotiation of time limits, is up to you. The point is, such negotiation *is* possible and *can* be successful. Its ultimate success is mostly a function of communication.

CHAPTER ELEVEN

Friends: Getting Them, Keeping Them, Losing Them

a good friend asked
what life would be like
if i lived as if i and others
had no past
and you had no history
all there is
is only what you and i
make up together . . .

When you think of an odd couple, do visions of Neil Simon's wonderful characters, Oscar and Felix, come to mind? If so, forget them! For much of society, the "odd couple" appears to be the partners in an age different relationship who have chosen something different from the generally accepted match-up, and who may be paying the price.

When we say "paying the price," we are referring to that arena of life in which we mix with other people, sorting and choosing, eventually ending up with a category called

133

"friends." But this group of people, these potential friends, do not always take as kindly to an age different couple as to one with a more conventional mix.

In both the written responses to surveys and the personal interviews we conducted, the subject of friends revealed some of the most diverse answers. Not necessarily from each couple as a unit, but from the individual partners.

"My friends thought Jonathan was super neat," gushed Joyce.

"The hell you say!" responded Jonathan. "I thought most of your girlfriends treated me like I had leprosy."

"Well, maybe at first, until they got used to the idea that I was involved with someone much older. But I think they all really like you," Joyce said.

We received similar responses from almost all the other couples. They perceived the reactions of their friends differently, and most were quick to point out that friends who were not intitally receptive "eventually came around."

Still, we didn't place all our trust in this data, knowing that many age different couples are cautious about exposing any apparent vulnerability in their relationship. The approval of family and friends is one of those vulnerable areas. When we pressed the point, we often heard, "Our friends were reluctant at first to accept our relationship, but then they came to accept it."

There are several reasons friends react this way:

1. They project fears from their own relationship on the age different couple.
2. Lack of common interests.
3. Ghost Partners from the past.
4. Continuing friendships with previous partners.
5. Peer pressure.

Let's examine each of these areas to look at the dynamic that is going on, and the effect on the age different couple.

1. Projecting Fears on the Age Different Couple We noted that female friends of the same age as their own spouses often react with an almost paranoid terror to being in the company of an older man and his younger female partner. It doesn't seem to matter how hard the female partner in the age different relationship may try to exhibit all the qualities that allowed her relationship with her older partner to flourish. She and her age different relationship are still often perceived as a threat to the other woman.

The unspoken fears of the other woman really boil down into one: "Could my mate leave me and take up with a younger woman?" Magazines and television shows are filled with this plotline, and it is applied to both famous and not-so-famous people. It is not only a common fear, but one that may appear to be justified when you look at divorce statistics and study the sociological data that tells us many men do leave their wives of many years for younger women.

Sociologists, psychologists, and therapists have dealt for years with these occurences, and for the most part have been content to label them manifestations of male menopause. The familiar story of the respected husband and father suddenly acknowledging a longstanding affair with a younger colleague, associate, student, or daughter of a friend has been told again and again, and will probably continue to be told.

It is unfortunate that one half of the age different couple equation (older man/younger woman) has to deal with this stereotype from the beginning in an attempt to continue friendships with female acquaintences. The threat the female friend may feel can be so strong that one may observe attempts by her to make sure her husband does not spend

135

too much time with the age different couple. After all, her thinking may go, he may get the idea that he might like to find a younger woman, too.

It's difficult to confront that kind of thinking, especially since it is rarely stated outright, but we have found that talking about the positive aspects of our relationship and staying away from any reference to trying to recapture lost youth or replace a parent works best.

Another common problem for the age different partners is how older friends often treat the younger spouse. A woman we interviewed named Vicky told us, "There was a long period of time—at least it seemed long—that Paul's friends treated me like a child. I could barely get a word in edgewise in any conversation, and I often left parties or gatherings feeling about six years old. I'm thirty-five. I've done a lot of things, and learned a great deal; I felt resentful that my opinion seemed so insignificant to them."

Paul concurred. "At first I thought Vic was being oversensitive. But after awhile, I began to notice the same thing. Then we made friends with another couple, one whose partners were almost exactly between our ages. They treated us so differently, as a couple and as individuals, that it was apparent something had been happening with my friends."

"I've since wondered if Paul's male friends felt envious, and their wives felt threatened," Vicky added. "I don't really know. I just know that we've lost friends who were important to Paul, and sometimes I feel responsible. Yet I don't know what I could have done differently."

Possibly Vicky could have, lightheartedly and with humor, said, "Hey, wait a minute! Just because I'm younger doesn't mean I can't add something of value to this conversation. What do I need to do to have you take me seriously?" You may want to use your own words, but the point is to confront your right to be accepted as an adult with valuable and interesting input.

In the case of an older female and younger male relationship, it often seems to be her friends who feel threatened. It may be her male friends and husbands of female friends who feel threatened, particularly sexually. They may perceive the older female partner as having dumped her husband to seek out a younger sexual partner. And if the male friend's sexual appetite has decreased, he may feel a sense of inferiority for not contributing as much to the sexual aspect of his own relationship as he thinks he should. This is brought up in his mind as he compares himself to what the younger man appears to be contributing to the age different relationship.

We laughed with all the couples who mentioned the reactions listed above, because we had to deal with some of them as well. Nevertheless, when you sense a friend is threatened by your relationship, their fears must be confronted, either directly or indirectly. All of our survey couples expressed confidence that such feelings existed among their friends, even if the feelings had not been openly expressed.

"I sensed my best friend was positive her husband was feeling threatened because I had my younger husband, and we were going places, doing things, and being active," Marilou said. "It was pretty obvious I had a glow. So many people would ask me what was going on with me, I seemed so different." Marilou *was* different. All during our interview, she acted like a woman in love, and that was the message coming through loud and clear.

In confronting these feelings of being threatened, it may help to remind friends of the circumstances of the relationship preceeding the age different one. Perhaps there had always been trouble in it—factors that were common knowledge in the past. If friends do not have the same serious problems in their own relationships, they need not feel their

AGE DIFFERENT RELATIONSHIPS

spouse would leave them for an age different partner. But when someone finds a new, younger partner, many of the genuine factors which led to the breakup of the past relationship slip from their friends' memories.

It is up to the age different couple to reinforce recognition of what has actually brought them together, and to point out the changes that have occurred in their lives as a result of these factors. Still, the younger female partner may have a difficult time securing a foothold with her older partner's female friends, since it is sometimes hard to overcome their feelings of insecurity.

And that's the key word—"insecurity." For the couple secure with the state of their own relationship, there is no threat from the age different relationships of others. A new friendship may take time and effort, but it can eventually ripen and be satisfying for all concerned.

2. Lack of Common Interests Any age different couple has come together because the partners have found some common interests they share. However, the friends from before they became a couple may still be involved in other interests of one of the partners. The topic of children may be the most glaring example of a lack of common interest.

When Allison and Brad talked with us, Allison told us the biggest drawback to their relationship, as far as she was concerned, was not having any children together.

Brad told us, "In my first marriage, I ended up with three kids to raise—my wife and our two children. In this relationship with Allison, who's older than I am, I like the fact she is mature and already established."

Allison told us that in spite of a difference in age, Brad fits in well with her old friends.

"Men my age seem so settled," she said. "Brad is very active, and wants to be doing things. But instead of that being a problem, it has inspired some of my older friends to try new and different activities, too. However, the fact I'm not a mother does get in the way sometimes."

At the root of Allison's regret is the fact that a woman who has had children and experienced the pleasures and pitfalls of parenthood often has a difficult time relating to a woman who does not have children. Maggie, by choice, has no children. Instead, she chose to concentrate on her career. Still, she told Cyn, she has made it a point to be enthusiastic about her husband's children, and the children of his friends.

"Even so," she said, "I feel this certain underlying uncertainty when I talk to them—what could I possibly know about raising kids? Or maybe it's more, 'how could I possibly understand their concerns and pressures?'"

Cyn asked how Maggie combatted this problem.

"I usually confront it openly. I say, 'You may not think I know what I'm talking about. But remember, I come from a family of four kids, so I had a real great background in childrearing, especially since I was the oldest'."

Besides the children/no children issue, other unshared interests can be big players in the age different couple's "friend hunt." When we were interviewing Billie and Herb, Billie, the older partner, admitted they didn't have many friends together.

"Herb plays a lot of softball," Billie said. "Last year he played one hundred and fifty games. That translates into four nights a week playing ball, with a tournament every weekend. Herb's friends all wanted to go out and party after the games. I just couldn't do that and still be up for my job the next day."

We wondered how they got beyond this problem, and asked, "What about *your* friends, Billie?"

"Well, Herb's always been attracted to older women. He gets along well with them, so my friends feel comfortable around him whenever he's available. However, he thinks he has a hard time talking to them."

"I have a hard time talking, period!" Herb said. "You don't know how tough it is for me to be talking to you two now," he added. "But I think Billie's friends know how much I love her, and how happy we are, and they accept me for what I am in her life."

So, several options are available to you as an age different couple and your friends. You can develop new shared interests or activities with them. You can confront behavior that causes you to feel uncomfortable. You can explore the possibility of developing new friends and including them in the circle you share with previous friends. And you can seek out other age different couples. All involved have the opportunity to grow.

3. Ghost Partners from the Past In any divorce or loss of a previous mate, there are residual effects. A number of the friends you now have are probably friends from a previous relationship of you or your spouse. Because of this, there are "ghosts" lingering in those old friendships, and as we told you in the chapter dealing with previous lovers, old ghosts have to be exorcised for a relationship to work. This is as true for a friendship as it is for a romantic relationship.

When a partner in an age different relationship introduces old friends to the new person in his or her life, eyebrows tend to elevate. You can almost hear the list of mental comparisons being compiled behind the smiling faces and handshakes. You and your new partner may have dreaded this "coming out," yet you want to be known as a couple to your friends.

With the age different component present, the appearance of the ghost partner from the old relationship is usually stronger and more obvious. Many times, couples told us about the open mention of the previous partner, as if the new partner were not even present.

140

"My God, I felt like I was just a fly on the wall," Ramona, the younger spouse of Frank, said. "My husband and his friends kept reminiscing about old times together, and I sat there like a bump on a log. It really pissed me off," she added with some emotion.

Frank added, "I was insensitive as hell to this until Mona finally had a good old-fashioned butt chewing with me about my behavior. Now I make sure I nip those kinds of conversations in the bud. I don't let them get started."

Ramona said, "The worst rebuff I had was when I would be talking, making some kind of point about something, and the other couple would just interrupt and go right on with their conversation, paying no attention to what I was saying."

"We are no longer friends with those people," Frank said. "And while it was sad for me to lose this longstanding relationship, I could see the other couple couldn't get rid of the ghost of my ex-wife. It was as if they were hoping to break up my relationship with Mona so the old gang could get back together again."

Ramona added, "We've met some new people through a bridge club we attend. They treat me totally differently. There is no history, and it's totally refreshing."

Ramona confronted the behavior making her uncomfortable—in this case, the behavior was her husband's. Frank recognized how he had contributed to her feelings and reaffirmed his loyalty to their relationship by confronting the behavior of his friends. In this case, his friends would not make changes. But we heard in our interviews that, in many other cases, friends of both age different partners did make more of an effort.

In almost all cases, we found the ghost partner problem with old friends to be tied into the next problem area.

4. Continuing Friendships with Previous Partners Admittedly, this is a difficult and sensitive area. Many people want to remain friends with ex-husbands or ex-wives of a partner in an age different relationship while trying to maintain friendships with the couple. It is very difficult, we found, to make this work. Inevitably, conversations drift to "something Harry or Alice said when I saw him/her last week." Then you have the ghost partner syndrome all over again.

At first, attempts may be made to overlook these references. However, if allowed to continue, they will get in the way of being able to maintain a truly rewarding friendship.

"I finally decided that we needed to help Frank's friends choose between us," Ramona said, continuing our interview. We asked how they had accomplished this without causing any hard feelings.

"Let me," Frank interjected. "These were my friends. In fact, the man who did this most was my best friend. I felt an enormous loss, and even some anger, that it had come to this. But I knew it wasn't working. Mona felt more and more left out and uncomfortable, and that was making me feel equally bad."

"So we just began to not initiate plans to see them, this other couple, for awhile," Ramona said. "But I could see Frank missed them, so I suggested we invite them to a party or two, although not so often as before. When we didn't hear from them, however, we could feel they were making their choice of friends."

"To tell you the truth, I'm relieved," Frank added. "It just wasn't worth it anymore. Mona and I are making new friends, as she said, with no previous history for us to deal with. It's much more rewarding for us as a couple."

We suggest the first approach in dealing with this problem area is to try to express your objections to your friends in a positive way. If that doesn't work, you need to "put the ball in their court" by saying, "What do you (or you two) think should happen for us to have a friendship?" If neither of these approaches work, the friend or other couple needs to experience the absence of you two from their life for a while. There's an old saying: "If you love something, let it go. If it comes back, it's yours. If it doesn't come back, it never was yours."

5. Peer Pressure This last stumbling block may seem relatively small at first glance. There is so much pressure from society at large focused against the age different couple that peer pressure from friends seems to be a minor difficulty in comparison. However, in this case the peer pressure is applied not to the couple as a unit, but to one or the other partner by his or her peers, and it usually involves doing things the way they have always been done in the past.

Since you have heard our strong message about the need for change for partners in an age different relationship, you probably can already see how the pressure to continue to do things "like we used to" can become unbearable at times. A longstanding relationship with the peer making such a demand makes the problem even tougher. The following scenario may sound familiar to you:

"Oh come on, John. Liz will love the Frank Sinatra concert. I'll pick up four tickets as soon as the box office opens."

"Well, I'm not so sure about that, Dave," says John. "She isn't really into that era like we are. But Chris Isaacs is in town that weekend, and I know Liz wants to see him in concert."

"Who the hell is Chris Isaacs?" asks bewildered but well-meaning Dave. "Come on, you can settle for the tickets with me later," he insists, applying the old peer pressure. "Ellen can hardly wait for Ole Blue Eyes!"

And so it goes—the more resistance you put up, the stronger the peer pressure becomes. The partner in the age different relationship seems to be faced with the choice of hurting old friends or fighting the pressure applied by them. However, the age different partner must stand their ground. Then, the couple wins, and those who lose their friendship by insisting on things being just like before give up something by their choice.

In the case cited above, John and Liz did go to the Sinatra concert, and while Liz's enthusiasm was not overwhelming, she was at least pleasantly surprised with the tickets and glad she had made the effort to go.

Both Dave and Ellen were ecstatic, of course, because Sinatra was their hero and their romantic link to an era when their relationship had first flourished. But when John then invited them to see Chris Isaacs, they refused.

"I don't think I'm interested in wasting the time and money on one of those rock and roll dingbats," Dave said bluntly in front of Liz.

She tried defending her taste in music, but realized she was talking to a brick wall, even though she had agreed to attend the Sinatra concert. To try to correct their impression about Chris Isaacs, or even to get this couple to see another point of view, turned out to be hopeless, although Liz's effort was commendable.

Liz and John then turned to a couple of Liz's generation and invited Toni and Pearce to go to the Isaacs concert. They were receptive to the idea, and accepted without hesitation.

John had some ticket connections and made the arrangements. Liz and Toni gathered some Chris Isaacs CDs, and John got a quick but thorough introduction to his music. The live concert turned out to be surprisingly enjoyable for John.

While Liz and John handled the situation well, there is no doubt that peer pressure can be damaging. It can force one of the partners to do things not to offend a peer, even when doing those things might rupture the jointly-held sense of dedication to the relationship that is required. This sense of dedication says, "We will do things differently and not be tied into doing what we did before just because friends want us to."

Forcing either partner into peer-pressured events or positions is contrary to the age different couple's creed of "change for the better." Better not to yield to peer pressure than to give a message to your partner that says, "Your wishes don't count when it comes to something my friends think we should do." To do so is a sure way of sabotaging your relationship.

Realize that engaging in an age different relationship may not be easy. This book is about taking risks and making changes. If you are involved in an age different relationship, you are committed to making changes. To do so is a transformational process; you, your partner, and your lives become different from the time before you made that decision.

During any process of transformation, sometimes people close to you cannot deal with the changes and choices you're making. This difficulty is often—perhaps always—something that is not easy to handle. We have no quick or easy answers.

Instead, we offer this challenge: the opportunity to find, nurture, commit to, and enjoy an age different relationship can be within your grasp if you will reach out to expand your options. Don't be bound by social convention, peer pressure, or what you think someone else will think about your choice.

Reach for the happiness that may be available to you in an age different relationship. Look at what can be *right* in such a relationship, rather than dwell on what is perceived to be wrong. An age different relationship is an alternative for you to consider for your own fulfillment and happiness. If you make such a choice, we are confident our ideas can guide and smooth your journey. That has been our goal.

145

Afterword
by Jack Mumey

Writing this book with my wife, Cynthia Tinsley, has been an experience unlike anything else. We had talked about this project for more than two years. Every time we would accomplish another goal, or leap over another barrier in the way of our relationship, we would ask each other, "What seems to make this work for us?"

Clearly, there were two elements that stood out. One was the fact we were dedicated to making the changes necessary in attitudes, lifestyles, and appreciation for each other. The second was that this was and is definitely the best relationship either of us has ever experienced; so much so that we are willing to constantly work at the nurturing necessary to keep this relationship strong and growing.

As I got into the heart of this book, a full understanding of the patience required within an age different relationship unfolded. Patience appears to be the collagen that holds it all together, and to that end I think both Cyn and I have had to expand our warehouse of patience with each other and with ourselves to let the whole process work.

Some of these chapters made us both acutely aware of how much work we do put into this relationship, how much more work than many same age couples we know. What is the reason for this? Simply put, as we have written, any age different couple starts with a demerit or two as far as the way society views us. There are times when paranoia about what others think about us is the ruling emotion.

What we learned as we wrote is that our relationship and our marriage forces us to work at it like no other relationship either of us has had before. And that's wonderful. Too often, as I deal with so many couples in therapy, I find the main ingredient in a failing or fracturing relationship is the desire to make changes, to work at building a new relationship to replace the one that has been allowed to die over the months or years of its life.

In an age different relationship, change is the driving force, and courage to change is the fuel. We have set our course and are proud of the way in which we continue to navigate and handle the twists and bends in the road, the detours and roadblocks that have been set before us, all with a vital energy that seems to rebound from one of us to the other with an uncanny sense of which partner needs it most at the time.

My adult children, daughters Tracey, Dana, and Dawn in the Denver area, and son Jackson in Florida, have all noticed and commented on this phenomenon to both Cyn and me. They have also been incredibly supportive of our relationship, something for which I love them and thank them.

I hope what you have read will allow you the freedom to choose, as Cyn and I have chosen, a different way of looking at relationships and an energetic way to deal with a difference in age. We also hope that it will help you make a difference in your lives by helping you develop and devote yourself to a satisfying union which continues to grow day by day.

Afterword
by Cynthia Tinsley

During the time we were writing this book, my grandmother died—shortly before Christmas 1992. I dedicate this
book, or the part of it I've written, to her and to my family.
She specifically left me two items in her will: a cedar chest,
and her desk. This woman kept eveything everyone ever gave
her. She knew all of us better, I often think, than we know
ourselves. There are no two things she could have given me
that could have been more appropriate.

My sister and I discussed at the funeral that neither she
nor I had ever specifically told our grandmother what our
interests were. Yet she knew somehow that what she left her
family was exactly perfect for each of us. I also keep everything everyone gives me, so a cedar chest is perfect for me.
And I write and work a lot (as my coauthor points out
frequently), so the desk is also perfect.

So, first I dedicate this book to my grandmother. All I've
ever wanted to do in my life is to write, and she was one of
those people who always, no matter what I was trying to do,

was totally supportive. And I believe she was so with every member of her family.

As I consider her passing, and mortality in general, I feel compelled to acknowledge the contribution of other people to my development as a person who has finally done what she always wanted to do.

Therefore, I dedicate this book to not only "Mommie," but also to my father, who taught me my work ethic. To my mother, who taught me how to be strong, to confront issues, and to use tools (an important contribution for someone who lived alone for a long time). To Granddaddy, who died several years ago, for my religious upbringing and my ability to be open-minded about philosophical issues. He is the one who read to me, which revealed to me the entire universe was available through reading. I cannot disregard "Poppie," my other grandfather, also gone these several years, a former policeman who called me "Monkey" and who always made me feel wanted. Nor can I leave out "Grandmommie," my other grandmother, a nurse who taught me by example how to cope with emergencies and, again, to be strong. She lives alone in her own home, still strong and independent, as Mommie did until the very end. And I cannot overlook my sister Kim, who taught me to do what I want to do—never mind what anyone else says. Finally, I have had the privilege of having ancestors who have been strong and independent. Members of my family have helped found cities in Texas.

The minister presiding at the funeral of my grandmother mentioned how much she loved to watch the Dallas Cowboys play football. She and I and my dad used to discuss why the Denver Broncos, the team I now follow (unless the Cowboys have a better season), couldn't quite make it all the way to a Superbowl win. She died early in the morning on one of the rare occasions when the Denver Broncos played the Dallas Cowboys. It was an excellent game. Difficult for me, because of divided loyalties, but it was exciting and unpredictable.

My grandmother lived her life valuing the qualities that made that game so special. She was open-minded to the end. She accepted everything that confronted her. She was aware and alert and intelligently conversant about current events until her last day, and she was 92 years old when she died.

I did not know until after the funeral that she was older than Poppie. I did not know until then that her first name was Winnie. I did not know that she fought the morphine the physicians were giving her for her pain because she wanted to be aware and alert to the end.

I want to live life like she did, which is why I dedicate my part of this book to Mommie and my family. This would not have happened without them, and I want them to know it.

My husband and coauthor, Jackson Mumey, deserves more credit that I can express. He has supported me through my continuing education and through many difficult times, eaten innumerable macaroni and cheese dinners, and has continually supported anything I felt I needed to do to grow and develop. He is my inspiration.

Thanks also to Duane and Dean, for contributing to the happiness of my parents. And to Ron, most recently, for contributing to my sister's happiness. Thanks more than I can adequately express to Tracey, Dawn, Dana, and Jackson, Jack's "children," for accepting me into their family.

To Winnie Lorene Tinsley, James Orwin Tinsley, and Hoyle Bowles; I'm certain they will hear my acknowledgment somehow—if there is any communication between this life and their present existence, they will know. And if not, they are a part of me, and *I* will know.

To the following people as well, I give my thanks: Laurene Bowles, Nancy Tinsley Earnest, Kim Tinsley, and Jim Tinsley. I love you.

151

Let us hear from you!

We would like to hear from you regarding this book and/ or your own experiences with age different relationships. Please write to us at the following address:

CYNJAC
3140-K South Peoria Street
Suite 430
Aurora, Colorado 80014

About the Authors

Jack Mumey is the author of six well known books, including *The Joy of Being Sober* and *Loving an Alcoholic*. His most recent title is *Sex and Sobriety*. Mr. Mumey is cofounder and owner of Gateway Treatment Center in Denver, Colorado, and is a state certified Senior Level Therapist. He is also in private practice.

Cynthia Tinsley has been a copywriter, layout and design editor, and copyeditor for a trade publisher. In addition, she has utilized education and work experiences to coordinate and present a number of seminars on behavioral communications, and is presently at work on a book concerning adult education. She and husband Jack Mumey live in Aurora, Colorado.